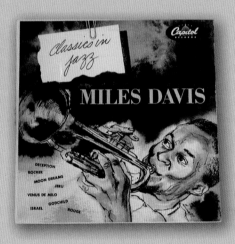

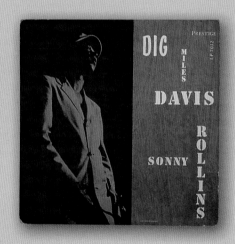

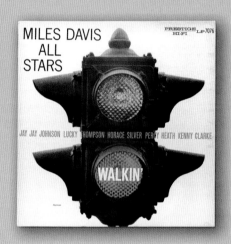

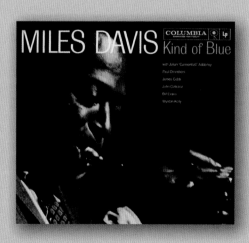

MILES DAVIS
the complete illustrated history

WITH **SONNY ROLLINS,** BILL COSBY, **HERBIE HANCOCK,** RON CARTER, **CLARK TERRY,** LENNY WHITE, **GREG TATE,** ASHLEY KAHN, **ROBIN D. G. KELLEY,** FRANCIS DAVIS, **GEORGE WEIN,** VINCENT BESSIÈRES, **GERALD EARLY,** NATE CHINEN, **NALINI JONES,** DAVE LIEBMAN, **GARTH CARTWRIGHT,** AND KARL HAGSTROM MILLER

Photographs from the archives of Francis Wolff, William Gottlieb, Bob Willoughby, William "PoPsie" Randolph, Lynn Goldsmith, and more

Voyageur Press

MILES DAVIS

Direction
SHAW ARTISTS CORPORATION
565 Fifth Avenue
New York 17, New York

Shaw Artists agency promotional portrait, circa 1955.

Contents

INTRODUCTION Running the Voodoo Down **6**

CHAPTER 1 THE YOUNG ARTIST 1926–1948 . . . . **10**
Beginnings by Ashley Kahn
There Was a Time . . . by Clark Terry

CHAPTER 2 BIRTH OF THE COOL 1949–1953 . . . . **40**
Miles in the 1940s and Early 1950s by Sonny Rollins
Miles and Style by Bill Cosby

CHAPTER 3 HARD BOP 1954–1958 . . . . **68**
Miles in France by Vincent Bessières
Love for Sale by Robin D. G. Kelley

CHAPTER 4 KIND OF BLUE 1958–1963 . . . . **94**
Miles, Newport, and the Business of Jazz by George Wein

CHAPTER 5 A NEW ENERGY 1964–1968 . . . . **120**
Miles and the 1960s Quintet by Ron Carter and Herbie Hancock
Miles and the Ballads by Francis Davis

CHAPTER 6 *BITCHES BREW* AND BEYOND 1969–1974 . . . . **142**
Miles, Tony Williams, and the Road to *Bitches Brew* by Lenny White
Miles Goes Acoustic by Karl Hagstrom Miller

CHAPTER 7 HIATUS AND RECOVERY 1975–1985 . . . . **176**
Miles and Women by Nalini Jones
Miles Davis in the Ring by Gerald Early

CHAPTER 8 *TUTU* AND FAREWELL 1986–1991 . . . . **192**
Miles in the 1980s by Greg Tate
Timing by Dave Liebman

AFTERWORD Miles in the Afterlife by Nate Chinen **214**

INDEX **220**

Running the Voodoo Down

MORE THAN TWENTY YEARS SINCE MILES DAVIS PASSED AWAY, this most maverick of musicians remains a huge force in the world's sonic and cultural landscape. Whether it's the casual fan who purchases *Kind of Blue* because they've been told it's good make-out music or the hardcore jazz fan who searches the globe for bootleg concert and studio recordings of Davis with certain ensembles, every listener responds to what the man with the horn brings to proceedings.

Miles Davis' place in the twentieth century artistic pantheon has long been assured. He is one of those rare individuals whose fame supersedes him. Indeed, to many in the general public, Miles *is* jazz—not because they listen to him above all others, but that he is the name they associate with a genre of (largely) African American, (largely) instrumental music in the same way that Leonardo da Vinci gets cited most often when the public are asked to name a famous painter. That Miles never had a hit record in the manner of Louis Armstrong or Herbie Hancock (even *Kind of Blue*'s domination of the back catalog album sales list is a relatively recent phenomenon) only goes to emphasize how huge a shadow he casts across jazz.

If this shadow consisted only of Miles' music then we could wonder at how his playing touched so many people. And, of course, it did touch—and continues to touch—millions of listeners across the world. But Miles' fame was based on much more than just music. For a small man Miles Davis cast a huge shadow, his very presence embodying all kinds of notions of "cool" and "blackness" when both those concepts were fresh and fraught. His supreme self-possession and disdain for what seemed like pretty much everyone else created an id of sorts than many others have since (unfortunately) emulated. His fearlessness when challenging the white American establishment—whether New York City police, record company executives, or racists who loathed seeing French beauty Juliette Gréco reclining in his arms—made him an icon of Black Power even if Davis was, for the most part, uninterested in politics, Miles being all about Miles. Even his serial descents into hard drug addiction only added a rather louche glamour to his public persona—journalists normally only interested in the travails of Keith Richards or Iggy Pop celebrated Miles as a trumpet-wielding "badass" junkie.

Miles jests, 1955. *Pictorial Press Ltd / Alamy*

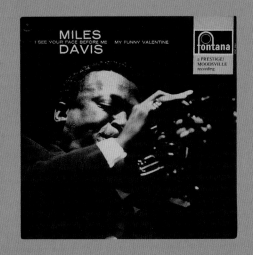
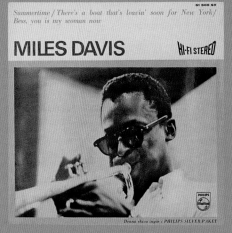

Miles became the stuff of myth while he was still alive. All kinds of titles were bestowed upon him both by observers and fellow musicians—"the Picasso of Jazz" and "the Prince of Darkness" being notably memorable. Trying to describe Miles and the sonic voodoo he created is like trying to hold flowing water. No matter, language will always struggle to suggest what music conveys. There were those who knew him personally and thus described not the music but the behavior. His son Gregory Davis wrote a trashy memoir about his father called *Dark Magus* and, undoubtedly, Miles did act like a monster at times. Yet whatever acts of ugliness he committed, the music of Miles Davis remains a testament to human imagination, emotion, and beauty. This does not mean that every note Miles played has artistic resonance—far from it: the forty-plus years he spent playing jazz are littered with misfires, second-rate performances, and some coldly cynical efforts. Yet the great body of Davis' work continues to fascinate and repay further listening.

For Miles Davis never simply rested on his laurels. Across his life, he pursued a relentless desire to challenge himself (and his listeners), and with his fierce vision and ability to surround himself with gifted young musicians he did so time and time again. In many ways he embodied the finest ideals of the United States—its energies and ability to constantly reinvent and start afresh and create what had never existed before. And, in his arrogance and excesses, he also embodied the nation's worst qualities. Critical as he was of American hypocrisies, Miles was very much an artist in the American grain.

I never got to meet Miles or see him in concert. All I have is the recordings, and they have fascinated me ever since I first came across a vinyl copy of *Kind of Blue*, its then cover featuring Miles blowing, biceps pumping out of a white singlet. It was a reissue cover fitting for the era of Rambo, but when I put the needle to vinyl the music that flowed out displayed such tender blues and soulful intelligence I've never stopped listening. Who, I wanted to know, could make such music? Where did he come from? Where is he going to?

Almost thirty years on I'm still asking those same questions. As, I believe, are all those who love to listen to Miles. This book then is a map of sorts to finding your way around the beauty, brutality, and brilliance of Miles Dewey Davis III.

GARTH CARTWRIGHT is an award-winning journalist and critic who regularly contributes to the *Guardian*, the *Sunday Times*, *fRoots*, and the BBC's website. He is the author of *Princes Amongst Men: Journeys with Gypsy Musicians* and *More Miles Than Money: Journeys Through American Music*.

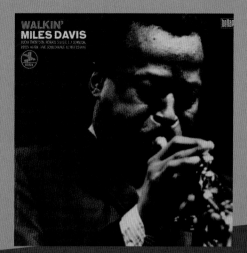

Poster, Belga Jazz Festival, Brussels, Belgium, October 29, 1987.

MILES DAVIS

1

The Young Artist

1926–1948

One of the earliest known photographs of Miles Davis performing onstage, circa 1947. *Michael Ochs Archives/Getty Images*

MILES DEWEY DAVIS III WAS BORN IN ALTON, ILLINOIS, on May 26, 1926. Alton sits on the Mississippi River, but, unlike many a seminal blues musician, young Miles would never know the cotton plantation and sharecropper's shack. Instead, he grew up in an upper middle class family, his father a dentist and, later, a gentleman farmer; his mother a haughty, piano-playing beauty; his uncles a journalist, an undertaker, a nationally known minister, and a president of the NAACP. Miles' father shifted the family to East St. Louis in 1929, aware that his dental practice could expand there, and Miles and his older sister Dorothy and younger brother Vernon grew up with a cook and maid on hand.

Not that life was always easy. Miles' parents fought incessantly (and sometimes violently), and racial discrimination still cast a bleak shadow across the city. St. Louis, while firmly located in the Midwest, was a Mississippi River city and thus home to many Southerners who shifted north looking for work. This meant the city played host to many remarkable musicians—the Texan ragtime pianist Scott Joplin lived there at the turn of the century and many a jazz and blues musician arrived on a riverboat, including Jelly Roll Morton and the young Louis Armstrong. And still, the violent racial intolerance that could be found in the Deep South also made its mark.

Postcard views of East St. Louis, Illinois.

MacArthur Bridge across Mississippi, from St. Louis to East St. Louis, Ill.

Wharf Scene from Bridge, East St. Louis, Ill.

Broadway, Looking East, East St. Louis, Ill.

From an early age Miles demonstrated character traits that stayed with him throughout his life: a passion for music, a love of fashion (his parents dressed smartly and ensured their children were also well turned out), a willingness to speak his mind, and an understanding that wealth made life easier. Of small stature, Miles focused his energies not on sports—although he shared a passion for boxing and was proud that his father had played golf with heavyweight champion Joe Louis—but upon learning trumpet. Aged ten, Miles declared he wanted to learn trumpet, as he liked how trumpet players looked while they held the instrument. Looking is one thing but learning is another, and Miles demonstrated the discipline necessary to master the instrument in a city already noted for its African American brass marching bands.

Miles began learning trumpet from African American educator Elwood C. Buchanan, a merciless disciplinarian. Determined to improve his technique, Miles then began crossing the Mississippi to St. Louis for a weekly half hour lesson with Joseph Gustat, principal trumpeter with the St. Louis Symphony. Gustat initially told Miles that he was the worst trumpet player he had ever heard, but the youth took this in stride and practiced even harder. Gustat insisted his pupils play without the then-fashionable vibrato, and this classical technique would pay off when the adult Miles developed his remarkably resonant trumpet tone.

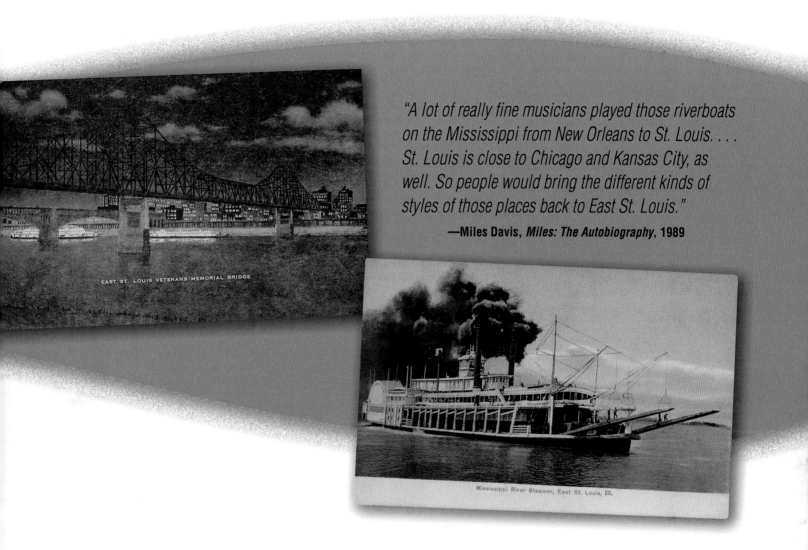

"A lot of really fine musicians played those riverboats on the Mississippi from New Orleans to St. Louis. . . . St. Louis is close to Chicago and Kansas City, as well. So people would bring the different kinds of styles of those places back to East St. Louis."

—Miles Davis, *Miles: The Autobiography*, 1989

EAST ST. LOUIS VETERANS MEMORIAL BRIDGE

Mississippi River Steamer, East St. Louis, Ill.

"I also remember how the music used to sound down there in Arkansas, when I was visiting my grandfather, especially at the Saturday night church. . . . I guess I was about six or seven. We'd be walking on these dark country roads at night and all of a sudden this music would seem to come out of nowhere, out of them spooking-looking trees that everybody said ghosts lived in. . . . I remember somebody would be playing a guitar the way B. B. King plays. And I remember a man and a women singing and talking about getting down! Shit, that music was something, especially that woman singing. But I think that kind of stuff stayed with me, you know what I mean? That kind of sound in music, that blues, church, back-road funk kind of thing, that southern, midwestern, rural sound and rhythm. I think it started getting into my blood on them spook-filled Arkansas back-roads after dark when the owls came out hooting."

—Miles Davis, *Miles: The Autobiography*, 1989

LOUIS ARMSTRONG

Associated Booking Corp.
JOE GLASER, President
New York, Chicago, Hollywood

Miles sought out new jazz 78s and played with friends in makeshift bands. In the 1930s, jazz was America's favorite dance music although, beyond Louis Armstrong and Duke Ellington, this generally meant the white bands led by the likes of Benny Goodman, Glenn Miller, Tommy Dorsey, and Gene Krupa. Black American tastes leaned more towards the funky jazz of Fats Waller and Cab Calloway, the exquisite pain of Billie Holiday, juke-joint blues, and gospel shouters. Urbane Miles recalled experiencing the latter formats as a child visiting his grandparents in rural Arkansas. "I guess I was about six or seven. We'd be walking on these dark country roads at night and all of a sudden this music would seem to come out of nowhere. . . . A man and a woman singing and talking about getting *down!* . . . That *kind* of sound in music, that blues, church back-road funk kind of thing. . . . So when I started taking lessons I might have already had some idea of what I wanted my music to sound like."

Classical technique, blues flavor, a huge sense of self-belief—the young artist was taking shape. Yet Miles was never a populist. While black America sent gutbucket blues singers like Roy Brown and Wynonie Harris up the R&B charts, Miles took refuge in bebop, an art music focused on technique and improvisation that appealed more to hipsters and intellectuals than the masses.

It's interesting to note that St. Louis' most famous musical son was also born in 1926: Chuck Berry's musical genius involved blending speedy hillbilly tunes with blues rhythms and witty narratives. Berry enjoyed none of Miles' privilege and, by the time he got to recording in 1955, he had already worked in factories and served a jail sentence for armed robbery. Did the two St. Louis masters ever meet? There's no record of it, and Miles never mentioned Chuck, whereas Berry, in his 1957 anthem "Rock And Roll Music," sang

I've got no kick against modern jazz,
Unless they try to play it too darn fast
And lose the beauty of the melody

The song suggests Berry had checked out bebop and was less than impressed. While the two St. Louis masters shared age, city, and race, they couldn't have been more different in other ways: Chuck was tall, self-contained, and a brilliant populist, while Miles was small, reliant on playing with select musicians, and an outsider. Yet both were visionaries who made a huge mark on modern music. A final, defining difference found Berry never varying from the format that made him famous while Davis constantly pushed his sound in different directions.

And it was Miles' ultimate decision to move beyond the orthodox bebop played by his mentors Dizzy Gillespie and Charlie Parker that would establish him in his own right.

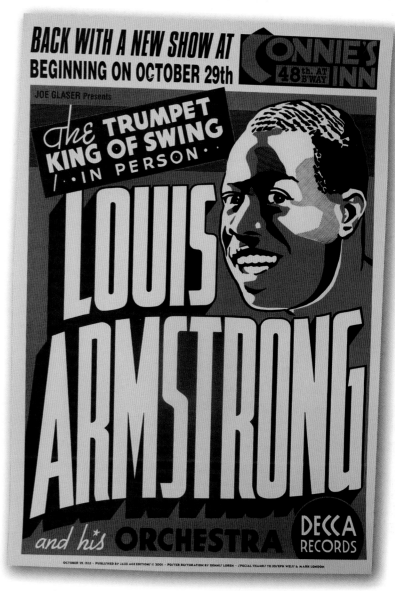

Louis Armstrong was not the first jazz cornet or trumpet player, but after he played his horn—in particular on the sides with his Hot Five and Hot Seven made in Chicago in the late 1920s—jazz would never be the same. He turned jazz into a soloist's art form where improvisation was king.

BEGINNINGS

by ASHLEY KAHN

ASHLEY KAHN is the author of the critically acclaimed books *Kind of Blue: The Making of the Miles Davis Masterpiece* and *A Love Supreme: The Story of John Coltrane's Signature Album*. He has earned three ASCAP/Deems Taylor awards and two Grammy nominations for his liner notes.

"In high school I was best in music class on the trumpet. I knew it and all the rest knew it—but all the contest first prizes went to the boys with blue eyes. It made me so mad I made up my mind to outdo anybody white on my horn. If I hadn't met that prejudice, I probably wouldn't have had as much drive in my work. I have thought about that a lot. I have thought that prejudice and curiousity have been responsible for what I have done in music."

—Miles Davis, the *Playboy* interview, 1962

There was a story Miles Davis liked to tell, and throughout his life, he told it often. During his brief three-semester course of study at the prestigious Juilliard School of Music, an instructor was explaining that the blues came from the pain and plight of the American negro. As Miles related in his autobiography: "She was up in front of the class saying that the reason black people played the blues was because they were poor and had to pick cotton. So they were sad and that's where the blues came from, their sadness. My hand went up in a flash and I stood up and said, 'I'm from East St. Louis and my father is rich, he's a dentist and I play the blues. My father didn't never pick no cotton and I didn't wake up this morning sad and start playing the blues. There's more to it than that.' " (*Miles: The Autobiography*, p. 59)

Never mind that the teenage trumpeter, then attending one of the country's leading conservatories in a decidedly more separate and unequal era, risked jeopardizing his good fortune. It's possible, in that one simple classroom exchange, to know volumes about the man who would change the future of music. Miles was abundantly self-aware and proud. He could be cocky and outspoken, with a confidence and intelligence beyond his years. He was sensitive— at times overly so—with an especially short fuse when it came to matters of music and racial stereotyping. He was adept at sizing up a person and would not hesitate putting them on the spot. It was a skill Miles perfected over time—one he would use for sport and self-protection, but that would also serve him well professionally, guiding him to famous musical partners, allowing him to draw the most from the celebrated groups that he would assemble.

Obviously, Miles was also given to brutal honesty. The personal circumstances he described to his nonplussed Juilliard instructor were all true, and had as much to do with shaping whom he was and what he became, as the city and the era into which he was born.

East St. Louis, facing St. Louis on the east coast of the Mississippi River, was a well-off, industry town offering steady employment and a vibrant cultural life in the first half of the twentieth century. It was well-known to African Americans—both notoriously, as the site of the country's bloodiest race riots in 1919, and more positively, for harboring a scene that was drenched in the sound of the Southern blues and jazz styles spinning north from New Orleans. During the height of the Jazz Age, East St. Louis was a primary destination for riverboats filled with dance bands, as well as touring orchestras. In 1927, a year after Miles Davis was born, Duke Ellington scored his first major hit with the tune "East St. Louis Toodle-Oo," drawing even more attention to the city.

He was named Miles Dewey Davis III by his father—a college-educated dentist who also ran a profitable pig farm—and his equally accomplished mother, Cleota Henry Davis, who played violin and once gave lessons on the organ. His birth date was May 26, 1926, and he grew up in a racially mixed, middle-class neighborhood in East St. Louis, walking distance to the river in one direction and his school in the other.

Miles received a strict upbringing; education was an unquestioned necessity, and a college degree was the goal. From his father—a proud and positive "race man" to use the parlance of the day—Miles learned to be racially aware and never look upon the color of his skin as a detriment. Miles credited his mother—with whom he often argued after reaching adolescence—for his independent spirit and taste in clothes. She also bestowed on him two 78rpm recordings, one each by Duke Ellington and Art Tatum, that he treasured.

Miles' earliest musical memories include the country blues and gospel he heard when visiting his paternal grandfather in rural Arkansas, and the popular black hits of his day that he caught on late night radio. By the early 1930s, that meant big bands and swing, the sounds of Fletcher Henderson and Louis Armstrong.

Miles played trumpet in the school bands. He is pictured here seated, sixth from the left in the back row.

"*Playing with Eddie Randle had to be one of the most important steps in my career. It was with Eddie Randle's band that I really started opening up with my playing, really got into writing and arranging music.*"
—**Miles Davis**, *Miles: The Autobiography*, **1989**

DANCE TO THE SOPHISTICATED RHYTHM OF

EDDIE RANDLE and his Blue DEVILS

For Booking Write 4214 W. N. Market St., Phone JE 1-2475, St. Louis, Mo.

Eddie Randle's Blue Devils (also known as the Rhumboogie Orchestra) were famed for their hot dance music in 1940s. The band made its home in St. Louis but performed at clubs throughout the area. Miles played with the Blue Devils for about a year when he was just 17. He is seated in the back row, far right, during a 1944 show at the Rhumboogie Club in the Elks Club in downtown St. Louis. *Frank Driggs Collection/Getty Images*

Even at an early age, Miles was blessed with a discerning ear. He prized more sophisticated styles over basic—though he never lost his taste for the blues—and musicianship over any other characteristic, racial or otherwise. "I could tell the difference between the sound of a black band and a white band," (*The Sound of Miles Davis* documentary) he would later say, while also acknowledging his taste for various trumpeters who happened to be white, like Harry James and Bobby Hackett.

By the age of twelve, music became Miles' primary focus and fortune smiled on his choice of instrument. His father bought him a trumpet over his mother's objections; she would have preferred he take up the violin.

A trumpet student during the 1930s could not have asked for a better locale than the St. Louis area—the city was already known for its rich tradition of brass players. All benefited from being just upriver from New Orleans; some had been schooled by a few German immigrants who had settled there, and shared a deep understanding of the instrument. As well, a healthy tradition of public parades led by marching bands both provided work opportunities for trumpeters, while cultivating the need for strength and endurance in their playing.

It also happened that a patient of Miles' father, Elwood Buchanan, was one of the leading music instructors in East St. Louis, and he happened to teach at Lincoln High School, where Miles had recently enrolled. Buchanan's influence had a major impact on the boy's musical start. He convinced him to avoid playing with a vibrato (part of Harry James' signature) and rather to develop a clear, mid-range tone on the trumpet. Miles then met the trumpeter Clark Terry, a close friend of Buchanan's, and he soon had a new hero to emulate and follow.

"The first time I heard Miles Davis, I had two choices. In fact all the guys in the band wanted to quit when I hired Miles. But I could see the possibilities, I said, 'Boy, the sky is the limit for this kid,' and the rest of them said, 'Well, you got a chance to get this other fellow with all this experience.' And I says, 'Well, he's got the experience and he's not going any further, he's like me. He just going to play good and that's it.' And I said sky is the limit for this young fellow. And so by being the boss, I didn't mean it exactly like that, but I didn't let them out talk me. And I was proud that I gave Miles the chance."

—Eddie Randle, 1971

"The greatest feeling I ever had in my life—with my clothes on—was when I first heard Diz and Bird together in St. Louis, Missouri, back in 1944. . . . Man, that shit was all up in my body. Music all up in my body, and that's what I wanted to hear."

—Miles Davis, *Miles: The Autobiography*, 1989

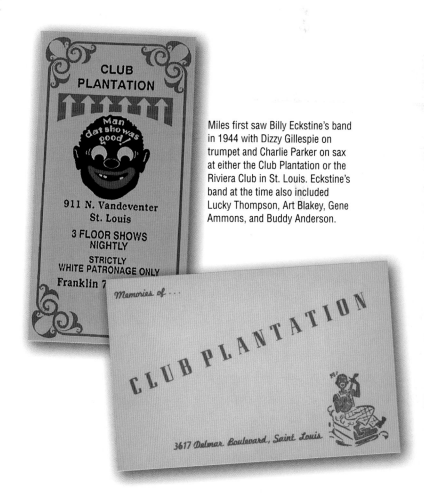

Miles first saw Billy Eckstine's band in 1944 with Dizzy Gillespie on trumpet and Charlie Parker on sax at either the Club Plantation or the Riviera Club in St. Louis. Eckstine's band at the time also included Lucky Thompson, Art Blakey, Gene Ammons, and Buddy Anderson.

BILLY ECKSTINE
and his Orchestra

XXXX
Exclusive Management
WILLIAM MORRIS AGENCY
NEW YORK   CHICAGO   LONDON   HOLLYWOOD

Bandleader Billy Eckstine—better known simply as "B"—circa 1944.

"B's band changed my life. I decided right then and there that I had to leave St. Louis and live in New York City where all these bad musicians were."

—Miles Davis, *Miles: The Autobiography*, 1989

"Dizzy was my idol then. I used to try to play every solo Diz played on that one album I had by him ["Woody'n You"]. But I liked Clark Terry, Buck Clayton, Harold Baker, Harry James, Bobby Hackett, and Roy Eldridge a lot, too. Roy was my idol on trumpet later. But in 1944 it was Diz."
—Miles Davis, *Miles: The Autobiography*, 1989

Dizzy Gillespie, circa 1946.

CHARLIE PARKER

GALE AGENCY. INC
48 West 48th Street
New York   N.Y.

"Back then Bird would play solos for eight bars. But the things he used in them eight bars was something else. He would just leave everybody else in the dust with his playing. Talk about me forgetting to play, I remember sometimes the other musicians would forget to come in one time because they was listening to Bird so much. They'd be standing up there on stage with their mouths wide open. Goddamn, Bird was playing some shit back then."

—Miles Davis, *Miles: The Autobiography*, 1989

Within four years, Miles was an up-and-coming member of the St. Louis music community, making his classes during the day, studying music in the afternoons and evenings, and playing pick-up gigs in bars and juke-joints on the weekends. An autodidact, he recalled an early onstage conversation that motivated him to teach himself chromatic scales and expand his repertoire.

"When I was about fifteen," Miles told writer Ben Sidran (*Talking Jazz*, p. 9–10), "a drummer I was playing a number with at the Castle Ballroom in Saint Louis—we had a ten-piece band, three trumpets, you know. He asked me, 'Little Davis, why don't you play what you did last night?' I said, 'What—what do you mean?' He said, 'You don't know what it is?' I said, 'No, what is it?' 'You were playing something coming out of the middle of the tune, and play it again.' I said, 'I don't know what I played.' He said, 'If you don't know what you're playing, then you ain't doing nothing.' Well, that hit me, like BAM! So I went and got everything, every book I could get to learn about theory."

Still somewhat shy, it took his girlfriend Irene—with whom Miles would eventually father three children—to call up a local bandleader and ask if her boyfriend could audition for an empty seat in the group.

Miles called his joining trumpeter Eddie Randle's Rhumboogie Orchestra (alternatively known as the Blue Devils) "one of the most important steps in my career." (*Miles: The Autobiography*, p. 42) Playing regular gigs with one of St. Louis' most established bands in one of the city's leading dancehalls exposed the young trumpeter to the company of professional musicians, many of whom offered tips and impromptu lessons. The experience provided him the chance to develop his trumpet playing, his composing and arranging. He eventually became Randle's musical director, setting up rehearsals and recruiting musicians, gaining the respect of many on the local scene, and national as well. Saxophonists Lester Young, Benny Carter and Sonny Stitt, trumpeters Kenny Dorham, Roy Eldridge and Fats Navarro were among the luminaries that Miles recalled meeting during his stint with Randle.

One night Clark Terry ran up to tell Miles how impressed he was by what he heard. "Yeah, motherfucker, you come up to me now saying that shit, when you wouldn't even talk to me when I first met you . . ." Miles recalled teasing his mentor. "We just laughed and have been great friends ever since." (*Miles: The Autobiography*, p. 43)

Miles was fast becoming his own man in every sense. In 1944, he graduated high school and became a father for the first time; though he and Irene were not married, he declared his intention to support her and the child. He also decided to travel to New York City and audition for Juilliard, though he would have to wait until that September (and despite his mother pushing him to attend Fisk University.) Biding his time, he continued playing with the Rhumboogie Orchestra, itching like most young men of his age to embark on the next phase of his life.

It was significant that Miles' stint with Randle lasted from 1943 to 1944, a pivotal period during which a number of social and cultural shifts were taking place on a national scale. The tide was turning in World War II—a conflict that the underage Miles was spared from participating in. With almost all eligible men in uniform, big bands like Randle's had been forced to lower the age of the musicians they'd consider, and when touring groups came through town, they would often look for local musicians to fill out their sections. Opportunities were rife for a young player in St. Louis with a union card.

Charlie Parker, circa 1946.

"Minton's was the ass-kicker back in those days for aspiring jazz musicians, not The Street like they're trying to make out today. It was Minton's where a musician really cut his teeth and then went downtown to The Street. Fifty-second Street was easy compared to what was happening up at Minton's. You went to 52nd to make money and be seen by the white music critics and white people."

—Miles Davis, *Miles: The Autobiography*, 1989

Minton's Playhouse on 118th Street in Harlem was ground zero for bebop. Standing in front of the club are Thelonious Monk, Howard McGhee, Roy Eldridge, and Teddy Hill in September 1947. *William P. Gottlieb Collection/Library of Congress*

Jazz fans dance away the night in Harlem. *Library of Congress*

Harlem was the center of the jazz universe in the 1940s at clubs such as Minton's Playhouse and Small's Paradise, as well as theaters such as the Savoy and Apollo. The daring new music hatched here was soon known as rebop or bebop.

OPPOSITE: Thelonious Monk experiments at the piano at Minton's in 1947. *William P. Gottlieb Collection/Library of Congress*

"That's what I was really in New York for, to suck up all I could from those sources; Juilliard was only a smokescreen, a stopover, a pretense I used to put me close to being around Bird and Diz. . . . Shit, I could learn more in one session at Minton's than it would take me two years to learn at Juilliard. . . . We was all trying to get our master's degrees and Ph.D.'s from Minton's University of Bebop under the tutelage of Professors Bird and Diz."

—Miles Davis, *Miles: The Autobiography*, 1989

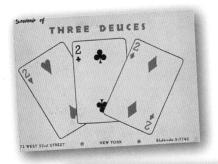

Manhattan's 52nd Street was known as "Swing Street" or simply, "The Street." It was home in the 1940s and early 1950s to jazz clubs such as the Three Deuces, the Onyx, Kelley's Stable, Club Samoa, and later, the Famous Door, Bop City, Birdland, and the Down Beat Club. *William P. Gottlieb Collection/ Library of Congress*

In addition, following its natural course, black music was evolving. In the early 1940s, a number of bands—led by the likes of Lionel Hampton and Louis Jordan—were developing a harder rhythmic edge, forging a dance-oriented hybrid that would lay the foundation of what would be dubbed rhythm and blues, or simply R&B, in the 1950s. Meanwhile, within the creative cauldron of a large band led by singer Billy Eckstine that also featured Sarah Vaughan and Art Blakey, a summit of musical sophistication had been scaled by alto saxophonist Charlie Parker and trumpeter Dizzy Gillespie, bending rhythmic convention with their jaw-dropping technique, daringly maneuvering through old song structures to create hip, new melodies.

In a flash, "Bird" and "Diz" became the new giants of this new black music. "Bebop" as the critics would soon label this new style for a post-nuclear age: frenetic and unpredictable, a soloist's art demanding close attention rather than politely fading into the background like other popular musical styles. It was the music that heralded the transition of jazz—a term only later applied generally to the tradition of improvised music that began in New Orleans speakeasies and bordellos—from functioning primarily as dance accompaniment, to its modern role as an art music.

When the Eckstine band swung through St. Louis in 1944 in need of a trumpeter, Miles was hired. Over the next two weeks, he was introduced to his future.

"After I had heard and played with Charlie Parker, Dizzy Gillespie . . . Art Blakey, Sarah Vaughan, and Mr. B himself, I knew I had to be in New York, where the action was," Miles later wrote. "I left East St. Louis for New York in early fall 1944. I had to pass my audition to get into Juilliard, and I passed it with flying colors. . . . Dizzy and Bird had told me to look them up if I ever came to the big Apple. I knew I had learned all I could from playing around St. Louis, knew it was time to move on. (*Miles: The Autobiography*, p. 49)

Was Juilliard simply a subterfuge by Miles to get his parents to pay his way to the jazz mecca that New York City has become by the 1940s? Not at first. With the confidence of youth, Miles arrived ready to learn it all and play with everybody, hungry for knowledge and experience.

Miles quickly found his footing in the New York music scene, and though it took a little longer, he found Charlie Parker as well. Miles was not alone in his quest, and when he finally had a chance to catch up with the saxophonist and join the line of initiates waiting to play with the leading figure of the modern jazz scene, Miles recalled it was less sitting in and more like an informal audition: "The first time I played [with Bird and Dizzy] I wasn't great but I was playing my ass off in the style that I played, which was different from Dizzy's, though I was influenced by his playing at this time. But people would watch for clues from Bird and Dizzy, and if they smiled when you finished playing, then that meant your playing was good." (*Miles: The Autobiography*, p. 60)

They smiled, and Miles began to play with them on a regular basis. When Diz was not there, Miles stepped in as the primary trumpet. He would play to the early morning then hustle back to his morning classes at Juilliard, where he would daydream about where he would catch Bird and Diz the next evening, planning where he could get a 50 cent bowl of soup to maintain his strength, and what clothes he would wear.

Photographs from this period show Miles dressed to impress, his still-skinny physique barely filling his sharp suits. In many, a wisp of a moustache is visible and he seems shadowed by his elders. To gain respect and project a no-nonsense maturity, he forged a tough-talking, street-wise persona. "Miles talks rough—you hear him use all kinds of rough words," Gillespie would later tell jazz historian Dan Morgenstern. "[But] his music reflects his true character . . . Miles is shy. He is super-shy. A lot of people don't believe that, but I have known him for a long, long time."

Diz in his trademark beret. *William P. Gottlieb Collection/Library of Congress*

"I knew everything Dizzy was playing. I think that's why Bird hired me—also because he wanted a different kind of trumpet sound. Some things Dizzy played I could play, and other things he played, I couldn't. So, I just didn't play those licks that I knew I couldn't play, because I realized early on that I had to have my own voice—whatever that voice was—on the instrument."

—Miles Davis, *Miles: The Autobiography*, 1989

Miles took over as Bird's trumpeter after Diz left the band—or after Diz kicked Bird out, depending on who's telling the tale. Dizzy was frustrated by Bird's unreliability and growing drug problems. Here, Miles plays alongside Bird at the Three Deuces in 1948 in a band including bassist Tommy Potter and pianist Duke Jordan, as well as drummer Max Roach. *William P. Gottlieb Collection/Library of Congress*

The Three Deuces glows under its crown of neon.
William P. Gottlieb Collection/Library of Congress

Gilbert J. Pinkus was the famous doorman for the Three Deuces and an all-round Swing Street ambassador. *William P. Gottlieb Collection/Library of Congress*

In addition to familiarizing himself with music theory, piano, and dictation at Juilliard, Miles soon learned the musical geography of the city. The majority of clubs—offering chances to work and jam—were on 52nd Street, or simply "The Street"; in Harlem, a number of bars and clubs provided more late-night opportunities to play and socialize. The differences between the two areas were easy to pick up. The Street attracted mostly white audiences made up of jazz devotees, dilettantes and tourists, and the music tended to vary widely, from traditional and swing-style jazz, to cabaret singers and bebop. Uptown the crowds were more focused on the performance and music was of a higher and more modern caliber, particularly at Minton's Playhouse where the ongoing development of bebop was truly in progress.

It was at Minton's that Bird introduced Miles to the house pianist, Thelonious Monk, whose harmonic innovations were codifying bebop, laying the groundwork for the entire modern jazz movement. Monk's use of space in his solos immediately influenced the young trumpeter; over time, their association would blossom and yield some of the most memorable music and historic moments of Miles' career.

Besides Monk, Miles befriended a number of like-minded, young musicians who were either recent arrivals or native New Yorkers. Together they formed what could be called the cult of bebop, all gravitating—like Miles—to Parker and/or Gillespie: drummers Max Roach, Kenny Clarke, and Art Blakey. Trumpeters Howard McGhee and Fats Navarro and trombonist J. J. Johnson. Bassists Oscar Pettiford and Curly Russell. Trumpeter Freddie Webster, who became Miles' fast friend and running buddy.

But it was with Bird that Miles hung tightest and most often—even allowing the saxophonist to move into his apartment, though his hero's addiction to narcotics and untidiness put Miles' temper and belongings at risk (when Irene arrived with their daughter Cheryl, Bird relocated.) Miles' hope was to not just play with him, but learn from him as well. Yet Bird was not a teacher in the traditional sense, as Miles recalls: "It was playing with Bird that really got my shit going. I could sit and talk, eat and hang out with Dizzy because he's such a nice guy. But Bird was a greedy motherfucker. We didn't never have too much to say to each other. We liked playing with each other and that was it. Bird didn't never *tell* you what to play. You learned from him by just watching him, picking up shit that he did. He never did talk about music much when you were alone with him." (*Miles: The Autobiography*, p. 64)

Miles could be describing himself as a bandleader. In years to come, every sideman who passed through the long succession of his ensembles would tell of his tight-lipped tutelage, of learning to play through a combination of intuition and intimidation, with little if any instruction. Though Miles would later credit Dizzy for speaking openly to him about music—explaining song structures, urging him to learn to play piano to better understand musical harmonies—it was his experience with Bird that would be most influential and career-shaping.

November, 1945: Miles had been hanging with Bird for just a year and was still attending Juilliard when he joined his idol in a studio just off Times Square to play on three of bebop's most legendary recordings, Parker's "Billie's Bounce," "Thrivin' on a Riff," and "Now's the Time." On the last tune, as Bird completes his solo, Miles famously enters, tentatively at first, then with increasing confidence, improvising a statement that is markedly different from the high-register trumpet flurries of Gillespie and other bebop acolytes: bluesy, free of embellishment, economically phrased. The seed of the style that would take Miles to the top had already sprouted.

By the midpoint of his sophomore year at Juilliard, it was clear to Miles and any of his instructors that his career was not going to be defined nor advanced by a college degree. He was devoting most of his time and energy hanging and making music on 52nd Street or uptown in Harlem. As 1945 drew to a close, Miles made another life-changing decision and returned home.

"I found at Juilliard that if I stayed any longer I was going to have to play like a white man," he later recalled, "because there were certain things you had to do, or a certain way you had to play to get in there, to be with them, and I didn't come all the way from St. Louis just to be with a white orchestra. [But] I had to go and tell my father that I was going to leave Juilliard. So I caught a train, and went into his office. He looked up and said, 'What the fuck are you doing here?' He was working on a patient . . . so when he got finished I said, 'This music is happening, Juilliard isn't, and I'm down on the street where everything's happening. More so, I'm learning more down there about what I want to do than at Juilliard.'. . . So I said, 'Save your money.' " (Ben Sidran, 1986)

With a warning to avoid sounding like everyone else—a superfluous admonishment if ever one was given—Miles' father bestowed his blessing. It was the last time the trumpeter would ask permission to determine his path.

SAVOY RECORDS

NOW'S THE TIME
(Charles Parker)
CHARLEY PARKER'S REE BOPPERS
Charles Parker, alto sax; Miles Davis
trumpet; Curley Russell, bass; Hen
Gates, piano; Max Roach, drums
573-B
(SAV-5851)
NOT LICENSED FOR RADIO BROADCAST - FOR W

SAVOY RECORDS

THRIVING ON A RIFF
(Chas. Parker, Jr.)
THE BE BOP BOYS
Charlie Parker, Alto Sax; Dizzy Gillespie
Piano; Miles Davis, Trumpet; Curley
Russell, Bass; Max Roach, Drums
Direction: Teddy Reig
945 B
(Sav. 5852) - FOR HOME
NOT LICENSED FOR RADIO BROADCAST

SAVOY RECORDS

STEEPLECHASE
(C. Parker)
CHARLIE PARKER'S ALL STARS
Chas. Parker, alto sax; Miles Davis, trumpet;
John Lewis, piano; Max Roache, drums;
Curley Russell, bass
Direction: T. Reig
937-A
(B 910)
BROADCAST - FOR HOME USE ON PHONOGRAPHS

SAVOY RECORDS

BUZZY
(Chas. Parker)
CHARLEY PARKER
with MILES DAVIS, trumpet
Bud Powell, Piano; Charlie Potter,
Bass; Max Roache, Drums
Direction - Teddy Reig
652-A
(S-3423)
BROADCAST - FOR HOME USE ON PHONOGRAPHS

SAVOY RECORDS

BILLIES BOUNCE
(Charles Parker)
CHARLEY PARKER'S REE BOPPERS
Charles Parker, alto sax; Miles Davis,
trumpet; Curley Russell, bass; Hen
Gates, piano; Max Roach, drums
573-A
(SAV-5850)
NOT LICENSED FOR RADIO BROADCAST - FOR HOME USE ON PHONOGRAPHS

DIAL RECORDS
Contemporary
American Music
1040-A
KLACTOVEEDSEDSTENE
CHARLIE PARKER QUINTET
CHARLIE PARKER_____Alto Sax
MILES DAVIS_____Trumpet
__E JORDAN_____Piano
__Y POTTER_____Bass
__ACH_____Drums
(D-1112)

SAVOY RECORDS

DONNA LEE
(Chas. Parker)
CHARLEY PARKER
with MILES DAVIS, trumpet
Bud Powell, Piano; Charlie P__
Bass; Max Roache, D__
Direction - Tedd__
652-__
(S-3__
NOT LICENSED FOR RADIO BROADC__

SAVOY RECORDS

(B 903)
PARKER'S MOOD
(Charlie Parker)
936 B
CHARLIE PARKER ALL STARS
Charlie Parker, Alto Sax; Miles Davis, Trumpet,
Bud Powell, Piano; Curley Russell, Bass;
Max Roach, Drums.
Direction : T. Reig.
EUROPEAN EDITION NOT LICENCED FOR RADIO BROADCAST

SAVOY RECORDS

WARMING UP A RIFF
(Chas. Parker, Jr.)
CHARLIE PARKER
and the BE BOP BOYS
945 A
(Sav. 5849) - FOR HOME USE ON PHONOGRA
NOT LICENSED FOR

SAVOY RECORDS

1589
BARBADOS
(Charlie Parker)
936 A
CHARLIE PARKER ALL STARS
Charlie Parker, Alto Sax; Miles Davis, Trumpet;
Bud Powel, Piano; Curley Russell, Bass;
Max Roach, Drums.
Direction : T. Reig
(B 900)
EUROPEAN EDITION NOT LICENCED FOR RADIO BROADCASTING

THERE WAS A *TIME . . .*

by CLARK TERRY

CLARK TERRY was mentored in learning trumpet by Louis Armstrong and in turn became Miles Davis' early mentor. He is one of the most prolific jazz musicians and most recorded trumpet players of all time, having appeared on more than 900 sessions. He has played with Count Basie, Duke Ellington, and Quincy Jones.

When you're playing a trumpet solo, the choice of notes is very important, and your style is going to determine the notes that you choose. If you like to play swiftly, you don't want to settle on any note, but if you like pretty notes, you find the notes that you can sustain and get something out of.

A lot of guys are different. Miles used to say to me, "Man, I like to start on the ninth." I couldn't make too much sense out of that. I said, "Why do you like to start on the ninth, Inky?" He said, "Because when I start on the ninth, I can go this way or that way." He must have had something in mind that he really wasn't explaining to me in the fashion that he understood. Then there's another thing he used to always say, "When I'm playing, I like to miss." I said, "Why do you like to miss?" He said, "Because if I attempt to make something, and I miss it, it makes the people wonder what I would have made if I had made that.'"

The mere fact that St. Louis is on the Mississippi River and these boats came up from New Orleans, it became a very integral part of jazz. A lot of the cats got off there and made it their home. St. Louis was always known for beautiful, fine ladies. That's a pretty good incentive. There was also good cooking and the places where they hung out had reasonably priced drinks. The rooms were reasonably priced. It just seems that St. Louis was a very inviting place.

The most sought-after gig at that time was a job on the Streckfus Steamers, which came up from New Orleans. The others were in the nightclubs: the Club Plantation, which catered only to Caucasians, and the Riviera, which was a black club. There were dance halls, like the Castle Ballroom and the St. Louis Finance. Aside from that, everything else was just little gigs which paid not a heck of a lot of money. There was a club called the Barrel—Jimmy Forrest stayed in there a lot, and I played there. The Hawaiians, a local watering hole where Roy Eldridge and Benny Carter and everybody that came to town would always end up, with sessions and so forth. There was an after-hours joint called Birdlong's which in the wee hours of the

morning everybody would pop into and drink until daybreak. That was about it. It was a small sphere of things that were happening.

There was a time in St. Louis that all the trumpet players were using mutes, because a lot of the clubs would require a softer type of playing. When you took out the stem, it just mellifluously cut the sound down to a different character altogether. It became a very popular thing. A lot of people think Miles started it, but cats were doing that in St. Louis long before Miles played a Harmon.

Most historians always refer to St. Louis trumpet players as a group of people who had a certain tradition, a certain sound, a certain background. I think it all stems from the cat who was the Lord Mayor of the whole situation named Charlie Creath who called himself the King of Cornet. I understand he was very dapper, fastidious, and a rambunctious, cocky type of cat, but I understand also that his playing could back up his attitude. All the cats wanted to swing like Charlie. We had our own group of trumpet players and all of these cats had something that hinged back to Charlie. There was Sleepy Tomlin, who was one of the first trumpet players that Jimmie Lunceford hired. There was Dud Bascomb, Shorty Baker, Levi Madison, and Dewey Jackson, who led a band called the Musical Ambassadors that was very popular in those days. And Miles Davis.

Miles credits me as being one of his influences, but there was only about six years difference in our ages. When I was twenty-one, he was still a teenager, and he sort of respected me. I was already a professional and Miles' teacher, Elwood Buchanan, would always tell me, "Man, you got to hear this little Dewey Davis. He's bad, man."

Elwood and I were old beer-drinking buddies. We'd drink this German beer—Griesedieck. People had other ways of expressing the name which you can imagine. I knew that Buch was a good trumpet teacher and had a heck of a reputation over in East St. Louis as a good educator.

Finally Buch got me to come over to East St. Louis, to Lincoln High School and meet this little skinny cat. He was skinny enough to ride a rooster, and if he'd have stood sideways, they'd have marked him absent. Miles was very shy. He'd look down when he was talking to you. But his father was a very successful dentist in East St. Louis, Dr. Davis, and this put him a position where he didn't have to take any crap from anybody. He came from money and this came out in his personality. He didn't give a damn about people, because people had been unkind to him, and possibly to his dad, who rose above the heap.

Miles used to love Harry James. Everything Miles played, he'd have a vibrato to it. Buch had a ruler with a piece of tape around it. He'd slap him and then say, "Stop shaking that note. You're going to shake enough when you get old." So between the use of a Heim mouthpiece and Buch slapping his knuckles, I'm sure that this had something to do with that pure talent for straight sound that he developed. Buch just was against him using a vibrato. He wanted a straight tone.

Shortly after that, Miles came down to Carbondale, Illinois, where I was playing with Benny Reid. We played the outdoor function for the Illinois interscholastic competition. Miles came up to me and said, can you show me something about something. I said, "Get out of here. I don't want to talk about no trumpet. You see all these pretty little girls bouncing around? They're looking good." He said, "OK."

We've laughed about this many times. The next time I saw him was at the Elks Club where the musicians would hang out and Eddie Randle and the Blue Devils played. Eddie was a trumpet player, and also an undertaker—Sykes Smith and Ernie Wilkins used to write for that band. I heard this trumpet I had never heard before. I ran up the stairs, and I'm looking there at this little skinny cat sitting there playing I said, "Man, that's good." He said, "Yeah, I'm the dude you fluffed off in Carbondale."

When I got to know him, we got to be real good friends. I feel very proud of the fact that in his book he mentions nice things about me. In fact I was one of the few people that he had some nice things to say about. I used to call him Inky. I don't know who nicknamed him that but not too many people called Miles Inky. He was very rich in color, and I asked him one time, "Miles, why they call you Inky?" Of course he would answer with a few choice words.

I used to chaperone Miles around to places like the Barrel, where we used to go and sit in and play, and a little place on Olive Street, across from the Tune Town Ballroom. And I used to find Miles mouthpieces. Joe Gustave was the first trumpet player of the St. Louis Symphony and all the people that he taught, he insisted on them using Heim mouthpieces, which are very curlicue and wafer-thin, almost thin as a coin. I never heard of them existing anywhere except in the St. Louis area. They were bowl-shape and curved on the outside, a beautiful design, but they were hard to come by. They were a little too thin for me. But a lot of cats played with them: Levi, Shorty Baker. Miles used to love these mouthpieces. Every time I'd find a couple of Heims, I'd take them to Miles.

Also at that time, I figured out a way of fixing the valve springs so they would respond quicker and be very light. Most valve springs were cumbersome and very difficult. Miles liked light springs—"brrrrrr"—so he could do that. He'd bring all of his horns to me, "Hey, man, fix my valves. You got any Heims for me?"

Miles played alongside bandleader Benny Carter at several stages in his career, including a short stint in Los Angeles in 1946. *William P. Gottlieb Collection/ Library of Congress*

In the period of *Bitches Brew*, I would say that Miles reached a point where he found that people would go for whatever they would go for and he would give it to them. Just to give you an idea: one time he was playing at the Village Gate during the psychedelic period. They had two areas where they had music simultaneously. Junior Mance was playing up at the bar. Miles was downstairs, where they got psychedelic lights and little kids running around and bouncing up and down.

We went down, me and Dizzy Gillespie, to catch Miles. He played this—I don't know whether you'd call it a set or tune or an experience, but it lasted for about forty-five or fifty minutes. It would change tempos and moods and dramatic scenery and psychedelic fixtures and all that. To me, it wasn't jazz; it wasn't the Miles I went down there to hear. I said, "Birks, I'm going to go upstairs and just listen to Junior Mance play some blues."

Finally they finished the experiment, experience or whatever. Birks came up, and then Miles comes up. He said, "Hey Clark. Hey Birks." Birks grabbed him and said, "I want you to tell me one thing. I know you know chords because I taught them to you. Now tell me, what the hell are you doing?"

It's hard to explain in words but this is the way Miles replied: he slapped his pocket—*bap, bap, bap*—and turned and walked away. "You know what I'm doing."

OPPOSITE: Miles joined veteran saxman Coleman Hawkins' band for a stand at the Three Deuces in 1947. *William P. Gottlieb Collection/Library of Congress*

Ernest Anderson presents
FRED ROBBINS'
ONE-NITE STAND
A Midnight Variety Concert
I'M SO TIRED

PEARL BAILEY
and the YARDBIRD of BEBOP

CHARLEY PARKER

Extra Added Attractions
BABS, 3 BIPS & A BOP
Eleven-Thirty Saturday Night
NOV. 29
At TOWN HALL

TONIGHT and EVERY NIGHT
New Bali
RESTAURANT
1901 14th St., N.W.
presents
CHARLIE
"BE-BOP"
PARKER
and his
ORCHESTRA
• Your Favorite Drinks
• Excellent Cuisine
• No Cover   • No Minimum
FOR RESERVATIONS—PHONE DU. 7544

ADM. 90¢
THE HOUSE THAT BOP BUILT
proudly presents
BILLY ECKSTINE
CHARLIE PARKER
and his band
SATURDAY MATINEES
4 to 6 P.M.
Circle 6-9559
THE Royal Roost
BROADWAY AT 47th ST.
Opp. Strand Thea.

HARLEM'S HIGH SPOT FOR COLORED SHOWS
125 ST. - 8" AVE
COOLED BY REFRIGERATION
APOLLO
Buddy JOHNSON
BAND & REVUE
— PLUS —
Charlie PARKER
and his BAND
BARGAIN MORNING SHOW 50¢ TO 12 NOON
WED NITE AMATEURS • SAT MIDNITE SHOW

BOB REISNER
presents
THE GREATEST IN MODERN JAZZ

"BIRD" CHARLIE PARKER AND HIS ALL STARS

SUNDAY, JAN. 9th

2 PERFORMANCES
Matinee: 5.30 to 7.30   Eve: 9.30 to 2 A.M.

OPEN DOOR
55 W. 3rd STREET

OPPOSITE: Leaving New York City behind for a time in 1946, Miles lived with Howard McGhee in Los Angeles while playing at a variety of clubs and in various bands. Like Diz and Miles, McGhee was one of the early bebop trumpet experimenters. Here, back in New York in 1947, Miles plays piano while McGhee blows his horn. *William P. Gottlieb Collection/Library of Congress*

2 Birth
of the Cool

1949-1953

Miles blows his horn onstage at Gene Norman's "Just Jazz" concert at the Shine Auditorium, Los Angeles, in 1950. *Bob Willoughby/Redferns/Getty Images*

NEW YORK PROVED EXACTLY the kind of musical melting pot Miles Davis needed. While his year studying at Julliard gave him a grounding in classical music theory, it was the hubbub of energy, ideas, and sounds pouring out of Manhattan's jazz clubs that both improved his technique but also allowed him to engage with likeminded individuals intent on pursuing a modernist musical vision. The time spent both observing and playing with the likes of Dizzy Gillespie and Charlie Parker carried Miles forward, allowing him to slowly carve out his own voice as a trumpet player—one who did not try and emulate Gillespie's speed, but instead tried to place his own softer, blue notes into the ensemble.

Bebop became something of a musical phenomenon. Its practitioners never sold many records but the U.S. media latched on to this radical new music (often offering ridicule) while many a young man dedicated themselves to emulating Diz or Bird—both musically and in other habits, sartorial and narcotic. Yet Miles never quite felt comfortable with a jazz devoted to furious flurries of notes. Perhaps it was the blues he recalled from childhood or simply his desire to go his own way, but by late 1948 Miles gave his notice to Parker. He was intent on making his own music.

MILES DAVIS

Direction
SHAW ARTISTS CORPORATION
565 Fifth Avenue
New York 17, New York

This was far from a simple task. To make the music he heard in his head, Miles needed musicians who shared his sound and vision. Fortunately, running in and out of New York jazz clubs were young musicians, both black and white, who also felt that the heat of bebop could be followed by something a little, well, *cooler*. Amongst them were Gerry Mulligan, John Lewis, Dave Lambert, John Carisi, and George Russell, all rising talents. These young men hovered around a 55th Street apartment where Gil Evans, a Canadian-born, veteran arranger with a great, lyrical passion for jazz, held gatherings. Ideas and sounds were thrown around, and Evans and Mulligan came up with the idea of a jazz nonet—a nine-piece little big band including such unlikely modern jazz instruments as tuba and French horn—that would forge the new jazz. If Evans and saxophonist Mulligan were the visionaries behind the nonet and provided (alongside Lewis) the bulk of the original material, it was Miles who, as Mulligan later acknowledged, "cracked the whip," taking things beyond talking, jamming, and dreaming.

Rehearsals found the young musicians excited at the sound they were creating. They employed the phrasing and drive of bebop; with Max Roach, bebop's ferocious drummer, laying down the rhythm it was unlikely they would break with the sound. Yet there was an elegiac quality to several of the compositions that reflected Gil Evans' desire to create epic arrangements and Miles' desire to forge a sense of space separate from bebop's rush.

With Miles already acknowledged as a rising star of the city's jazz scene the Nonet was booked to support Count Basie's big band across two September weekends at the Royal Roost, then one of New York's finest jazz clubs. Basie led a swinging big band that had won national and international fame across the previous decade and, upon hearing Miles' Nonet, Basie announced himself impressed—where bebop had alienated many older jazz musicians, what Davis' band was playing appeared more approachable. A Capitol Records A&R man also took note and signed Miles to record twelve songs for the then-fledgling independent label.

Mike Zwerin, a young white trombone player, was approached by Miles to attend a rehearsal for what turned out to be the Royal Roost band. While Zwerin was not part of the studio band that January, he later recalled of the rehearsals: "Miles was . . . cool. Pleasant, relaxed, diffident. It was his first time as leader, he relied on Gil. He must have picked up his famous salty act sometime later because he was sweet then." Zwerin admitted that he did not appreciate the Royal Roost concerts as historic or legendary: "A good jazz gig, yes, but there were others."

Published as part of the Be-Bop Piano Series in 1949, Miles' "Nuclear Fission" was never recorded by him.

Things with the Nonet progressed slowly. The audience at the Royal Roost had received them politely but with little fanfare, and the Nonet did not play in public again until late the next year. They did not enter the studio until January 21, 1949. The four titles they cut that day—"Move," "Jeru," "Budo," and "Godchild"—were released a few weeks later on two ten-inch 78s. Almost immediately these recordings proved a hit amongst New York's jazz cognoscenti, with musicians, fans, and critics alike all praising the new sound.

That Miles' name was on the 78 as bandleader later would be a source of some consternation to baritone saxophonist Gerry Mulligan who had both helped birth (with Gil Evans) the idea of a nonet playing a cooler jazz and written several of the compositions played. But Miles was already a more established musician and, as he would remain for the rest of his life, a figurehead, a man whose very presence attracted attention.

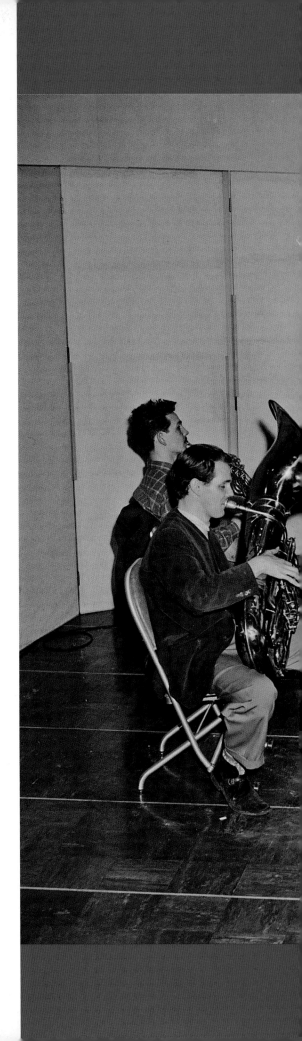

"I looked at the group like it was a choir. . . . I wanted the instruments to sound like human voices, and they did."

—**Miles Davis**, ***Miles: The Autobiography***, **1989**

Miles' Nonet records at Capitol Records in New York City on January 21, 1949, during the sessions that were eventually compiled and released on the *Birth of the Cool* LP. Clockwise from left: Bill Barber, Junior Collins, Kai Winding, drummer Max Roach (obscured behind the sound screen), Al Haig at the piano, Joe Shulman (standing at rear), Miles, Lee Konitz, and Gerry Mulligan. *William "PoPsie" Randolph/www.PoPsiePhotos.com*

Miles reviews charts with pianist Al Haig during the *Birth of the Cool* recording sessions. *William "PoPsie" Randolph/www.PoPsiePhotos.com*

Beyond attracting praise, little else changed in Miles' immediate life. He went back to playing in Charlie Parker's Quintet and subbed for Fats Navarro in a larger group.

Capitol invited the Nonet back into the studio on April 22, 1949, and Miles assembled the musicians with five substitutions. This time they cut "Venus de Milo," "Boplicity," "Israel," and "Rouge." Again, a positive response greeted the sophomore 78, but Miles had other things going on.

In May, 1949, he left the United States for the first time to play in Paris. There he found himself treated like royalty and was startled by the audience's response; Parisians had developed a passion for jazz almost from the music's beginnings. Striking up a relationship with actress-singer and existentalist muse Juliette Gréco made Miles the hippest man in Paris. Back in New York, he found himself at loose ends, people liking his music yet not so much that there was demand for him to lead a band. He took work backing Billy Eckstine and Billie Holiday and drifted, for the first time, into heroin addiction.

Having witnessed heroin wreak havoc on Charlie Parker, one wonders why Miles wanted to risk similar hurt. While playing in Los Angeles, he was busted for narcotics: This was an extremely serious charge, carrying not only the threat of imprisonment but a possible revoking of his New York cabaret card, thus making him unemployable in Manhattan. Fortune smiled on Miles—as it often would—and he was acquitted in January 1950.

Back in New York, Miles regrouped the Nonet and entered the studio for the little big band's third and final session on March 9, 1950. Here they recorded "Moon Dreams," "Deception," "Rocker," and "Darn That Dream," the latter featuring Kenny Hagood on vocals (easily the least accomplished of all the Nonet's recordings). Again, the resulting 78 received a positive response. But sales were minimal, and Capitol did not renew Miles' contract. The three 78s were not just admired but truly studied by other musicians, their influence rippling from New York out and across the United States (and, not too much later, into Europe and beyond).

"I was looking for a vehicle where I could solo more in the style that I was hearing. My music was a little slower and not so intense as Bird's. My conversations with Gil [Evans] about experimenting with more subtle voicing and shit were exciting to me."

—Miles Davis, *Miles: The Autobiography*, 1989

Horn trio during the *Birth of the Cool* sessions: Miles, Lee Konitz, and Gerry Mulligan. *William "PoPsie" Randolph/www.PoPsiePhotos.com*

"I remember one time when I hired Lee Konitz, some colored cats bitched a lot about me hiring an ofay in my band when Negroes didn't have work. I said if a cat could play like Lee, I would hire him, I didn't give a damn if he was green and had red breath."

—Miles Davis, the *Playboy* interview, 1962

Miles blows a solo during the
Birth of the Cool sessions.
William "PoPsie" Randolph/www.
PoPsiePhotos.com

great collections of popular songs

iles returned to leading sextets, signing to and recording for Prestige and then Blue Note across 1951–1953, yet heroin addiction cramped his talent and nothing from these recordings matched what he had cut for Capitol. Miles also worked as trumpet-for-hire, his main concern being neither his music nor his growing family but feeding what had become a monster addiction.

In 1954 Capitol gathered eight of the Nonet's recordings onto a ten-inch LP as part of their *Classics of Jazz* series. This helped spread the gospel of the new jazz as practiced by Miles Davis. Yet even before that mini-album came out, the influence of the Nonet's recordings could be heard: Gerry Mulligan, having shifted to Los Angeles in search of work, formed a piano-less quartet with Chet Baker in the fall of 1952. Baker, from Oklahoma, played trumpet in a manner very much influenced by Miles and sang ballads in a cracked, rather flat voice. This and his striking features—he resembled a hillbilly James Dean—led to almost instant success. Trumpeter-arranger Shorty Rogers began making arrangements for the Stan Kenton Orchestra that were influenced by Miles' Nonet recordings. Rogers' small group, the Giants, would also explore the new jazz while Nonet pianist John Lewis formed the Modern Jazz Quartet, further extending what he had helped create with Miles.

Ironically, Miles' Nonet recordings of 1949–1950 became legendary when, in February 1957, Capitol packaged all eleven of the Nonet's instrumental recordings on a twelve-inch LP under the title by which they've been known ever since—*Birth of the Cool*. The LP format was beginning to take off and modern jazz had become the unofficial soundtrack to abstract art, Beat poets, Harlem hipsters, anti-A-bomb protesters, students, and everyone else who didn't want to be "square." By then Miles was already becoming something of an icon—hip, beautiful, and supremely *cool*, that noun now loaded with meaning. Thus *Birth of the Cool*, almost a decade old and its music already vastly influential, became modernist America's soundtrack.

"Birth of the Cool became a collector's item, I think, out of a reaction to Bird and Dizzy's music. Bird and Diz played this hip, real fast thing, and if you weren't a fast listener, you couldn't catch the humor or the feeling in their music. Their music sound wasn't sweet, and it didn't have harmonic lines that you could easily hum out on the street with your girlfriend trying to get over with a kiss. Bebop didn't have the humanity of Duke Ellington . . . Birth of the Cool came from black music roots. It came from Duke Ellington."

—Miles Davis, *Miles: The Autobiography*, 1989

There was an irony in the literal and current figurative use of the term "cool" here. As writer Pete Welding noted, "the Miles Davis Nonet was anything but cool. Controlled, lucid, tightly focused, succinct, yes. It is all these and more, but cool in the sense of being dispassionate or otherwise lacking in the fundamental emotional character one always associates with the best jazz, no! As anyone familiar with the nonet's music can attest, it possesses an abundance of focused emotional power all the more effective for being so low-keyed, so apparently subdued in character."

By 1957, Miles Davis had achieved a comfortable level of fame but *Birth of the Cool* gave him greater kudos. These recordings attest to many things: How complete Miles' vision was at twenty-two, how eloquently he could express himself, the importance of Gil Evans as an arranger of music to Miles, and Miles' ability to bring out the best in his bandmates.

Yet at the end of 1953, Miles Davis was a heroin addict who stole from his fellow musicians, relied on his wealthy father for weekly allowance, ignored his partner Irene Cawthorn and their three children, and had made little music of note since his last Capitol session almost four years previously. Amongst jazz's cognoscenti many wrote him off as washed up.

In 1954, Miles would begin a remarkable comeback.

MILES IN THE 1940s AND EARLY 1950s

by SONNY ROLLINS

SONNY ROLLINS is one of the most influential jazz tenor saxophonists of all time. Among many others, he has played with Charlie Parker, Art Blakey, Clifford Brown, Max Roach, and Thelonious Monk as well as Miles Davis.

I first encountered Miles Davis as a sideman with Charlie Parker. Of course Charlie Parker was our god so to speak and Miles Davis was at his side, coming up underneath him, so that helped put him in the spotlight. I remember that my very good childhood friend Lowell Lewis, who was trumpet player in our band, really loved Miles' playing. He was in the band that I had with Jackie McLean, Kenny Drew, and Andy Kirk Jr. Once when we were rehearsing, I took a solo and was able to manipulate the time and it caught his attention, like he thought I was on to something. I remember later doing the same thing with Miles, and he stopped and looked at me the same way.

I thought it was very interesting that Miles played a different role than the great Dizzy Gillespie. Whereas Dizzy and Bird were playing in the same style in a sense, Miles came up with a contrasting way of playing. I mean he didn't just go the way that a lot of people were going. He had his own approach. I always liked Miles better than his contemporaries, like the great Fats Navarro. When I think about Miles' great solo on Bird's "Billie's Bounce" in 1945, in contrast to what else was happening at the time—it was perfect. So he was a big hero of mine and I empathized with his style.

I may be off by a few months but I'm pretty sure I first came to play with Miles in 1948. I was playing down at Minton's Playhouse, when they used to have a lot of jam sessions there, and one of the guys in the audience came to me after we played and said, "Hey, you sounded OK, kid. You want to play intermission at this club up in the Bronx, Club 845?" I knew about the place because every Sunday they had jam sessions there that had all of the stars of jazz, like Eddie "Lockjaw" Davis, Dexter Gordon, Bud Powell, and of course Miles Davis. All the big boys dropped by. So of course I said, "Great! I'll come up and play intermission."

At that time I had a trio, which consisted of myself, piano, and drums, which was unusual at the time but I always liked playing with a sparse rhythm section. There were a lot of changes going on with music at the time. Even after I got with Miles, we liked to play with the piano laying out; he called it a "stroll," like strolling down the avenue. That would become a feature at some point of a variety of songs that

we'd do, and of course it became a big part of what I've been doing all my career, the idea of playing with the barest of instruments, just bass and drums, which I found would still give me the propulsion and the freedom. It probably stems from the fact that when I started out I used to play to myself in the bedroom for hours and hours, in my reverie. Later on, I'd like to go out to the oceanside, in the park, any place and just play.

So when Miles first heard me it was with minimal accompaniment. He was one of the stars with the main group. He heard me playing and said, "Oh man, Sonny, I want you to join my band." The rest is history, as they say.

Miles was not someone who told you what to play. If you were playing with him, and he asked you to do that, then he already knew what you could do and what you sounded like. I mean we did work on numbers, but it wasn't like he told anyone what to play on it once we had it together. He gave us the freedom to be who we were. He wouldn't have hired you in the first place if he wanted something different.

When Miles used Jackie and me on his [Prestige] sessions, it was a sort of answer to the West Coast, cool sound that he had helped develop first with people like Gerry Mulligan and Lee Konitz. What we were doing was a sharp turn away from that direction. Some people saw it in a "white jazz" versus "black jazz" way.

Miles is great. I still have the same opinion of him now as when I first heard him. He was a seeker, which was evident from his early work with Charlie Parker. I read someplace that Miles said that the reason he changed his style as the years went on is because as he got older, he wasn't able to play as he did in the 1940s and 1950s. He changed to keep active even though he got a lot of flack from people who were disappointed he didn't keep playing the way that they liked.

I think there's also a philosophical reason for changing. Miles was a person who didn't want to be a relic; he always wanted to be moving with the times. I share that trait with him. I want to keep contemporary and I have a great love of music myself and we want to keep active, and if you're able to do that, that's beautiful. Some

Miles and saxophonist Sonny Rollins perform together at the New York Jazz Festival. *Bob Parent/Hulton Archive/Getty Images*

"People loved Sonny Rollins up in Harlem and everywhere else. He was a legend, almost a god to a lot of the younger musicians. Some thought he was playing the saxophone on the level of Bird. I know one thing—he was close. He was an aggressive, innovative player who always had fresh musical ideas."

—Miles Davis, *Miles: The Autobiography*, 1989

people can just be what they are and live their whole career like that, and that's beautiful too, but I'm not a good enough musician to be able to play one way all my life. This is a very complicated topic but Miles and I discussed this several times in different ways and we agreed mainly that things are always changing and that if you're able to assimilate the change it's better that way for people like us. I can't recreate something I did in 1950. I'm not that kind of musician and I don't think Miles was either.

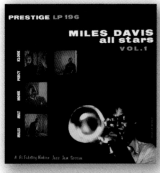
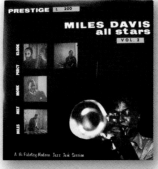

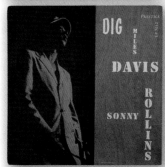

"I liked what I played on Dig, *because my sound was really becoming my own thing. I wasn't sounding like nobody else . . ."*

—Miles Davis, *Miles: The Autobiography*, 1989

Jackie McLean accompanies Miles during a Blue Note recording session at WOR Studios in New York City for the Miles Davis Sextet sessions on May 9, 1952.
Francis Wolff/Mosaic Images/Corbis

MILES AND STYLE

by BILL COSBY

Comedian, actor, author, television producer, educator, musician, and activist **BILL COSBY** was a fan and later, friend of Miles Davis.

Word went out: the Miles Davis Quintet is coming to town! Me and my boys have been waiting. We're excited. We get to the Showboat early, pick our seats, talk about the band and the latest album. We talk about the band members by their first names. Then suddenly they're on stage and they count it off "uh, uh, uh . . ." and they hit! You hear that first note and we all go . . . [closes eyes] Deep into the music.

When you're a fan and you really love somebody and think they're cool, you just want to walk in their shadow. I'm sitting with my boys after the set, talking and watching. At the Showboat, there were stairs going upstairs, past the bar, and Miles was sitting by himself on the steps. It just built up to the point where I couldn't help myself. I went up the stairs and sat right near him, just me and Miles. Me and Miles sitting on the steps—yeah.

He didn't leave, he didn't do anything. I mean I've come this far, but I don't know what to do. I'm having a conversation with myself, and it's not going very well. "Well, what are you going to say now? You got to say something to him." "We've got to think of something hip." "Well I don't know anything hip, what are *you* going to say to him?" "How about, you are *bad*, man. Your playing is mean." "No don't say that."

So I end up turning around and saying, "Everything going alright, isn't it?" and immediately I kind of cringed. But he said, "Yeah."

Now I got a problem because everything was built around being cool. How to leave and still look cool? I'm thinking, "Can't stay here forever. He's not talking and I'm not talking." So finally I get up and said, "I'll see you later Miles." He said, "Alright." Then I walk back to my boys, and they of course start asking, "What he say?"

"Oh we were just talking, man."

"Naah, we were watching you. You didn't say nothing. You didn't say *nothing*."

"Me and Miles . . ."

"Yeah. right, you and Miles. You and Miles what? What did he say?"

"He told me everything was fine and asked me where I lived. He told me he might come up and visit me sometime."

I was born in 1937 so by 1954 you can figure out how old I was. I was underage—you had to be twenty-one in Pennsylvania to get into a club to hear some jazz. In Philadelphia, we had two big clubs: there was Pep's, and right across the street was the Showboat in the basement of a small hotel. The thing for me was the matinee on Sundays that went from four to six or something like that.

So I'd paint on a little moustache, take a dollar to get in plus the fare to get there on the subway and back. I'd give the guy a dollar at the door, get this tall, smoked glass with a soft drink, no alcohol. And I'd just stand there and of course I'd get thirsty through three sets holding on to my one drink. Now the bartender was Freddie Tolbert, the guy Miles named the song "Freddie Freeloader" for. He was a hard guy, man. He didn't care if you were young, or broke. "Hey you, come on, get another drink!" I'd have my hand covering the fact that there was nothing in the glass. "No man, I'm still drinking!"

In those days—1954 and on—all of the great groups would come to town: Miles, Max, Blakey, Sonny. It was the hippest thing: they all had the same olive green, polished cotton jackets and slacks, with a white shirt and tie—all of them dressed the same. As teenagers we copied the way these guys dressed. In the project community those ivy-league suits were very, very popular.

Miles was certainly the person we copied the most: the way he dressed, the way he acted, the way he was, just being cool. If you had stack of eleven LPs and you were going to go to this young lady's house and you had to ride public transportation, you would put on the same clothes Miles wore, or as close as you could. And on top of the stack so people could see it, you would put Miles' latest LP. That's how important he was to us.

See in those days you didn't wait for the radio stations to tell you something was out, you just went to the store and you said, "Anything new?" You'd just get it and put it on. Albums were $2.49, and if it was Miles, it didn't matter. I had to have it.

OPPOSITE: Miles solos with the Metronome Jazz All-Stars in the MGM studios. *William "PoPsie" Randolph/www.PoPsiePhotos.com*

With his trumpet ready, Miles waits backstage before
Gene Norman's "Just Jazz" concert at the Shine
Auditorium, Los Angeles, on September 15, 1950.
Bob Willoughby/Redferns/Getty Images

Miles records with the Metronome Jazz All-Stars in New York City on January 23, 1951. Clockwise from bottom left: guitarist Billy Bauer, trombonist Kai Winding, baritone saxophonist Serge Chaloff, clarinettist John La Porta, alto saxophonist Lee Konitz, tenor saxophonist Stan Getz, and Miles. *William "PoPsie" Randolph/ www.PoPsiePhotos.com*

I remember that with Miles my parents never said, "Don't you already have that record?" I mean, there were quite a few musicians when I would play their latest LP, my parents would say that, but never with Miles. We were all able to come together; he connected with everybody. My mother, who just loved to dance to Jimmie Lunceford and Count Basie, she loved Miles' groups—she loved their beat and the fact that it wasn't screechy. She always said, "It seems like they have a plan."

There's one point about Miles that I'm sure everyone agrees on. He could play some piercing things that meant romance, that meant sex. He had a wonderful sense of foreplay with his horn, using silence so well—the space, the pause. He knew how to let you enjoy what he had just played. Women would hear this and love it, it was palatable. At the same time Miles could made hardened men shout with some of his breaks. On some tunes, you could *feel* that there was a promise of going into 4/4 coming off of 2/4 time—and then he would hit it.

You could call us a gang, me and the guys I used to hang around with, but it was nothing about beating anybody up. What we were serious about was jazz. It was very, very important for us to learn Miles' solos off of any recording, and then be the first who could stand on the corner and run it off from memory. I remember "Blue Haze," Part 1 and 2, were on a jukebox in our neighborhood and it cost 5 cents to play. It featured Percy Heath, Horace Silver, Art Blakey and Miles Davis. We all knew the parts, so if there were four of us, we'd say "OK, you be Percy." "You be Horace." "I'll be Miles." And we could scat the solos. To this day, I still know those parts, even Art's press roll.

We followed everything Miles did. Somebody would put out the word, "Philly Joe's not with them." And this would be before Miles was even due to come to town—the news came down to us from somewhere. "What?" "Yeah man." "Well, that's it, 'cause Philly Joe kept that stuff together." "Philly Joe's being replaced by some cat named Jimmy Cobb. He used to play with Sarah." "How you gonna have a cat who played with a woman singer, play with Miles? Miles is gonna run him off the stand." Then it was, "You know Red Garland's leaving the band." "What?" "Yeah." "Well this band's going to go bad now, man 'cause Red's . . ." "Yeah, they're getting some cat named Bill Evans. I don't think he'll be able to hang with Miles. I don't know why he did that."

Then the band would come to Philadelphia and blow everybody away. We realized that every time he made a change, it was right. He knew what he was doing.

Many years later, my wife Camille and I were in the south of France, and we went to see him at a concert in Cimiez, near Nice, I think this was five years before he died. He was in great shape. He's got this band now that's plugged in, and I'm loving it because Miles was teaching them how to really play the blues, showing them that you could leave notes out, how to mix the rhythms around, like he did on *Bitches Brew*. Some people may not have liked it but I loved what he was doing with it, man.

After it's over his manager comes out and says, "Miles says why don't you come on back?" I mean, even though I am now *the* Bill Cosby, I'll still tell people in a minute, "Miles Davis knows me." We went in and Miles is standing there, he had his shirt off with a towel around his neck, drinking a Coca-Cola and he's supposed to be diabetic. I know Cicely is going to kill him. So we're talking and somebody opens the door and looking out we can see there's a rope—about twenty-five feet away—with maybe fifty to seventy people jam-packed behind it wanting to come backstage. "Hey Miles!" "Hey, great show!" "Hey Miles!"

Then the door closed and Miles didn't even turn to us, he just said, "They've come to get what's left." It wasn't sad—it was just hip. "They've come to get what's left."

Miles and Lee Konitz join forces during the Metronome All-Star sessions.
William "PoPsie" Randolph/www.PoPsiePhotos.com

Miles and Stan Getz confer during a break in the Metronome All-Star sessions.
William "PoPsie" Randolph/www.PoPsiePhotos.com

OPPOSITE: Perched on a chair back, Miles plays with the Metronome All-Stars.
William "PoPsie" Randolph/www.PoPsiePhotos.com

Miles takes a break during the Metronome All-Star sessions.
William "PoPsie" Randolph/www.PoPsiePhotos.com

MILES DAVIS NONET
Arrangements by Gerry Mulligan,
Gil Evans, and John Lewis.

OPPOSITE: Bassist Percy Heath looks on as Miles notates a melody during a Miles Davis Sextet recording session for Blue Note in New York City on April 20, 1953. *Francis Wolff/Mosaic Images/Corbis*

3

Hard
Bop

1954–1958

IN LATE 1953, MILES DAVIS WAS AT A NADIR. He rarely played clubs outside of New York's Birdland and the handful of ten-inch LPs he had recorded for independent jazz label Prestige failed to convey the major talent that the Capitol recordings of 1949–1950 had so strongly expressed. Miles was in his late twenties and, voices whispered, washed up.

What had happened to the Miles who burned so brightly across the three Capitol 78s? A simple answer: Heroin addiction had derailed Miles to the point where he could not keep a band together let alone focus on creating groundbreaking new music.

Miles tried to kick heroin several times, often traveling home to St. Louis where he would go cold turkey in a cottage on his father's farm. Yet moving amongst a world of drug-addicted musicians, dealers, and acolytes meant temptation was always there. Inevitably, Miles slipped back into using. Throughout the early 1950s, he experienced much humiliation due to his addictions—once, turning up at his father's surgery and screaming for money, Davis Sr. rang the local police and had his son arrested. In later life Miles would look back on these years boastfully, as if being a junkie was a badge of pride, even boasting that he kept himself going by working as a pimp. "Had me seven women back when I was strung out in them old days," he told British rock writer Nick Kent in 1986, and Kent, like a lot of journalists who reveled in Miles as the Dark Prince, ate it up. Miles liked to romanticize his life, and while he did accept handouts from admiring prostitutes (and wealthy lovers), he lacked the iron determination and cold brutality a ghetto pimp employs to survive. Just as gangsta rappers like to tell stretchers about how bad they are, so did the rich kid from St. Louis.

Miles listens to a playback during a recording session in 1955. *Pictorial Press Ltd/Alamy*

MILES DAVIS

Contact: JACK WHITTEMORE
80 Park Avenue, N.Y.C.
(212) 986-6854

Promotional photograph, circa 1955. *Michael Ochs Archives/Getty Images*

Beyond his craving for heroin, Miles retained a great desire to play jazz. And as he observed several of his contemporaries winning far greater fame and fortune than he had yet achieved, this sparked a renewed desire in him for recognition. What surely aggravated Miles most was seeing how several West Coast musicians had taken on elements of his Capitol recordings and developed "cool jazz" out of it. That one of these "arrivistes" was former Nonet saxophonist Gerry Mulligan did not placate Davis, especially as Mulligan's co-conspirator trumpeter Chet Baker had become something of a teen idol. Mulligan and Baker shared Miles' chronic heroin addiction—Mulligan would serve six months in jail in late 1952 whereas Baker's enslavement to opiates would soon destroy his career. Yet when Miles was booked for a week's worth of concerts in May 1954 to support Baker's band at Birdland, the New York jazz club run by gangsters and one of the few places that still booked Miles, it fired Davis' competitive instincts. No way was he going to let a white boy who copied his style bask in Big Apple glory.

By now Miles had developed the taciturn personality that would mark him as one of the world's least approachable entertainers, and he froze out Baker and his band during their Birdland sojourn. The teenyboppers who packed Birdland to scream at Chet paid Miles little attention, but the New York critics crucified Baker while championing Davis. Emboldened, Miles finally got a handle on his habit. Whether he completely cleaned up is debatable, but from then on he was in control again and reengaged in making remarkable music.

Having met pianist Horace Silver, Miles put together a superlative sextet and they focused on creating a sound that would be labeled "hard bop." Hard bop's practitioners shared a belief in modern jazz as a voice for African American artistic and social expression. Bebop had radically broken with the past; Charlie Parker even took to claiming his music was "not jazz." But the hard boppers wanted to emphasize their music's connections with earlier black musical forms—blues, R&B, gospel—so continuing a dialogue that stretched back to slavery while looking towards the then-burgeoning Civil Rights movement. This was a music that the jazz writer and poet LeRoi Jones (later Amiri Baraka) would describe as "the anti-assimilationist sound."

On March 29, 1954, the Miles Davis Sextet drove to New Jersey to record for Prestige. Using a borrowed trumpet, Miles launched into "Walkin'," a blues he played with great clarity and determination. The other musicians were equally inspired and took superlative solos. They also recorded at that session a Dizzy Gillespie composition, "Blue 'n' Boogie." Everyone involved in the session—including producer Bob Weinstock—recognized that they had captured something remarkable, and, today, both tunes are hailed as contemporary classics. Once Prestige issued the recordings, they were championed as signaling the emergence of hard bop as a reaction to cool jazz's reserve. Here bebop was reassembled in a more recognizable and funky manner with a strong blues flavor. While African Americans remained, on the whole, much more enthusiastic about rhythm and blues artists, hard bop was a statement of racial pride that let the largely white, West Coast cool jazz musicians know the stakes were raised and they would not find easy entry to this club.

A June 1954 recording session with saxophonist Sonny Rollins featured Miles using the Harmon mute for the first time on record, thus creating a new sound for jazz trumpet. At a December 1955 session, Miles soloed so exquisitely on "Bags' Grove" that jazz writer Whitney Balliett was inspired to describe his trumpet playing "like a man walking on eggshells."

In early 1955, Miles was arrested for non-payment of child support and locked up in Riker's Island prison. While imprisoned, he heard news of Charlie Parker's death at the age of thirty-five. Parker's chronic drug and alcohol addictions meant his friends knew his time on earth was limited and Miles, showing a venom that he would become notorious for, sneered that Parker's death was due to his "greediness."

Advertisement, Syria Mosque, Pittsburgh, Pennsylvania, 1950s.

With John Coltrane at his side, Miles was reinvigorated. Here, the duo performs at Birdland in New York City on October 18, 1955. *William "PoPsie" Randolph/www. PoPsiePhotos.com*

"I knew that this guy [John Coltrane] was a bad motherfucker who was just the voice I needed on tenor to set off my voice. . . . And faster than I could have imagined, the music that we were playing together was just unbelievable. It was so bad that it used to send chills through me at night, and it did that same thing to the audiences, too. Man, the shit we were playing in a short time was scary, so scary that I used to pinch myself to see if I was really there."

—Miles Davis, *Miles: The Autobiography*, **1989**

The Newport Jazz Festival in Rhode Island was in its second year in 1955; Miles was not initially booked to play but he convinced festival organizer George Wein that he should be on the bill. Wein complied, adding Miles to a set featuring Gerry Mulligan, Zoot Sims, and Thelonious Monk. Miles took the stage dressed in a white sport coat and black bow tie, jammed his trumpet against the microphone to ensure he was the loudest musician onstage and played several fierce solos. In Miles mythology, this one performance of three numbers is what introduced him to a wide, general audience and convinced Columbia Records to sign him. His performance was indeed impressive—the shiftless junkie of recent years had been replaced by a focused and formidable player. Yet Miles had been chasing George Avakian of Columbia since 1952. Avakian recognized Miles' potential, but noted that Miles was signed to Prestige until 1957. Bob Weinstock of Prestige suggested that Miles record both for Prestige and Columbia, and a deal was worked out.

Miles insisted that he record with his new group: saxophonist Sonny Rollins, pianist Red Garland, drummer Philly Joe Jones, and bassist Paul Chambers. Yet the maverick Rollins declined to commit, and Miles approached Julian "Cannonball" Adderley, only to be told by Adderley that he had a teaching job in Florida instead. Miles then rehearsed with John Gilmore, a tenor sax player with Sun Ra's Arkestra, but found Gilmore's playing too radical. So Philly Joe Jones put in a call to a sax player named John Coltrane who had yet to make much of a name for himself.

Pairing John Coltrane with Miles Davis made for one of the great partnerships in jazz. Although born only a few months apart, the two men had little in common. Coltrane grew up in a working-class North Carolina household and lost his father while a child. He enlisted in the U.S. Navy in 1945, and embraced bebop after seeing Charlie Parker play in 1947. He had little interest in fashion or womanizing while suffering chronic addictions to alcohol and opiates. This didn't impress the reformed Davis but meant Coltrane fitted well with the other members of the quintet—Garland, Jones, and Chambers all being addicts.

Miles knew that hiring Coltrane was a risk—the saxophonist blew huge, raw blasts that Ira Gitler would call "sheets of sound" and divided listeners. Those who wanted modern jazz to be as radical as possible saw Coltrane as leader of the vanguard while others described his sound as alienating. Even Bob Weinstock was taken aback by Coltrane when the quintet entered the studio to record for Prestige. Miles, when challenged by Weinstock about Coltrane, recalled replying, "Man, just record the shit. You want us to play, we'll play. If not we'll go home." Miles explained later, "Trane was a big thing to be dropping on people! That was hard shit to just think of!"

That Miles saw in Coltrane a sparring partner who would push his music forward reflects on how determined the trumpeter was to take chances, to go for the radical direction rather than the safe one. Being back in the public eye—*Down Beat* magazine's readers voted Miles Best Trumpeter that year, tied with Dizzy Gillespie—and signed to a major label only served to feed Davis' hunger to achieve greatness. Now that Charlie Parker was dead, many fans expected Miles to take his place on modern jazz's throne. Indeed, he would, but not by playing it safe. Employing Coltrane signaled that Davis had nailed his colors to hard bop.

Another dramatic 1955 development involved an operation on Miles' throat to remove polyps. While recovering Miles began speaking too soon and permanently damaged his voice, leaving the harsh whisper that many would find made the trumpeter even more intimidating.

Intimidating *and* intense. Across three recording sessions in November 1955 and May and October 1956, the Quintet recorded thirty-one tunes that would go on to fill five Prestige albums: *Miles*, *Workin'*, *Streamin'*, *Relaxin'*, and *Cookin'*. The intensity of these first-take recordings replicates what the quintet must have sounded like live—the rhythm section, powered by Jones' magnificent drumming, pushes Miles and Coltrane forward, both sonic explorers, listening to and playing off one another, these two very different-sounding horn players caught up in the white heat of creativity.

Miles performs with saxophonist Lester Young as part of the Birdland All Stars during a tour of Europe in autumn 1956. *Michael Ochs Archives/Getty Images*

OPPOSITE: Miles, pianist Red Garland, drummer Philly Joe Jones, and bassist Paul Chambers record as part of the Miles Davis Quintet during the *Cookin'* sessions in New York City on May 11, 1956. *Michael Ochs Archives/ Getty Images*

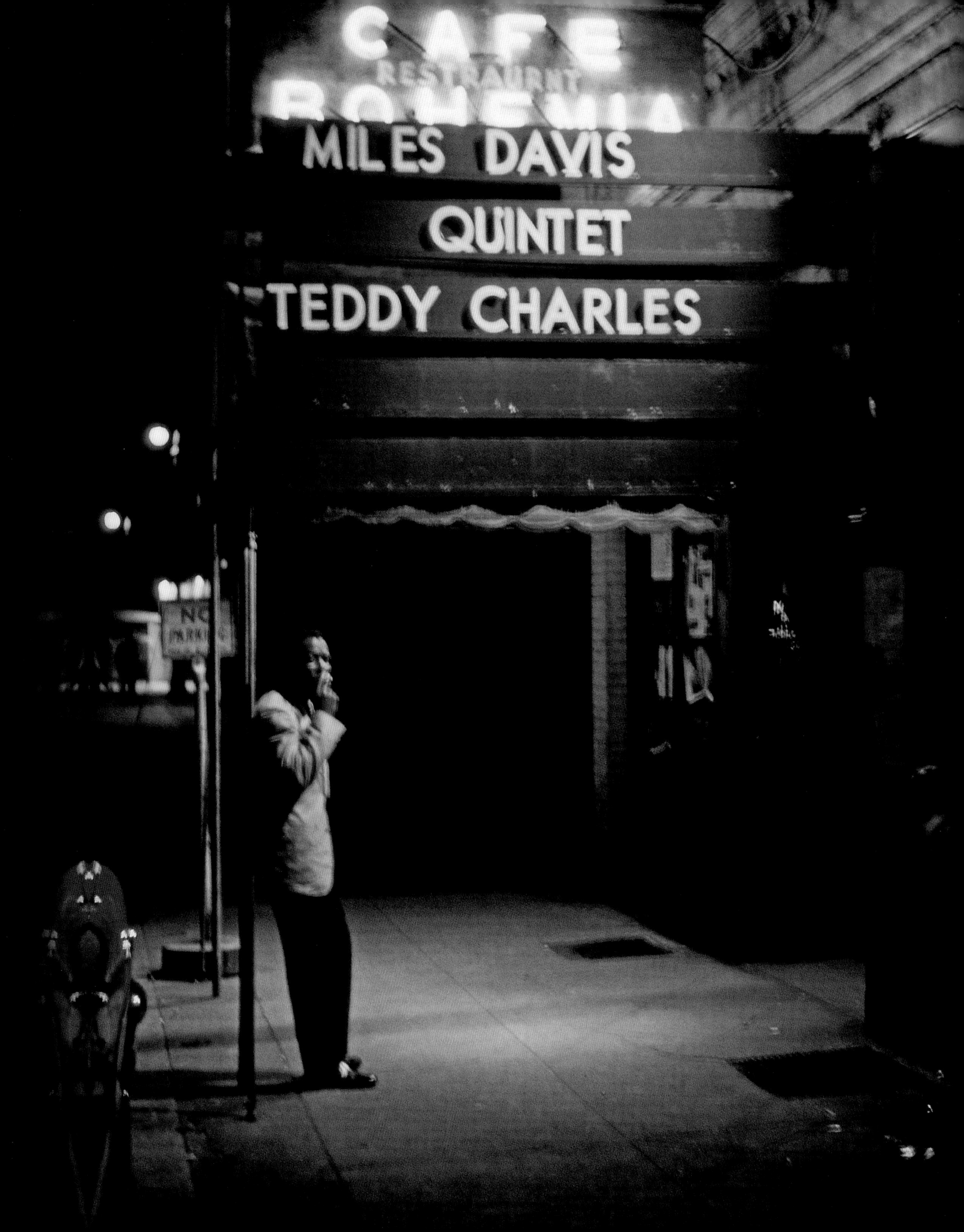
CAFE
RESTAURANT
MILES DAVIS
QUINTET
TEDDY CHARLES

The Prestige recordings appeared to exorcise Miles' hard bop demons as the quintet's first album for Columbia, 'Round About Midnight, explored cooler, more melodic jazz. Released in 1957, the cover featured an aloof Miles wearing shades and a sharp jacket, cradling his trumpet, bathed in an expressionistic red lighting on the bandstand at Café Bohemia in Greenwich Village, very much an icon of hipster cool. 'Round About Midnight would outsell all of Miles' seven Prestige albums combined, demonstrating both the strength of Columbia's marketing machine and the potentially vast audience for a melodic Miles Davis.

During April 1957, Miles fired both Coltrane and Jones due to their erratic behavior: Coltrane would, on occasion, nod off on the bandstand. Miles was, again, ready for a change and

when Columbia suggested Miles reunite with Gil Evans, he leapt at the idea. Evans arranged ten numbers, and across five days in May and August 1957, Davis played flugelhorn while backed by a nineteen-piece orchestra. The resulting album, Miles Ahead, looked back to what Davis and Evans had recorded for Capitol while pushing their concept of a symphonic jazz forward. Released in November 1957, Miles Ahead proved a huge success, its lush, almost languid tone establishing Davis as a musician whose appeal could reach a public who brought large numbers of Dave Brubeck and Frank Sinatra albums.

At the end of 1957, Miles returned to tour France and, whilst there, was commissioned to record the soundtrack for director Louis Malle's noir film, Ascenseur pour l'échafaud, which was released in the United States and Great Britain under various titles, including Elevator to the Gallows, Lift to the Scaffold, and Frantic. The film may be forgettable, but Miles' improvised score possessed remarkable atmospherics, his trumpet painting eerie tone poems, hinting at what lay ahead.

OPPOSITE: Miles smokes a cigarette under the marquee of the Café Bohemia jazz club in Greenwich Village, New York, in 1956. *Marvin Koner/Corbis*

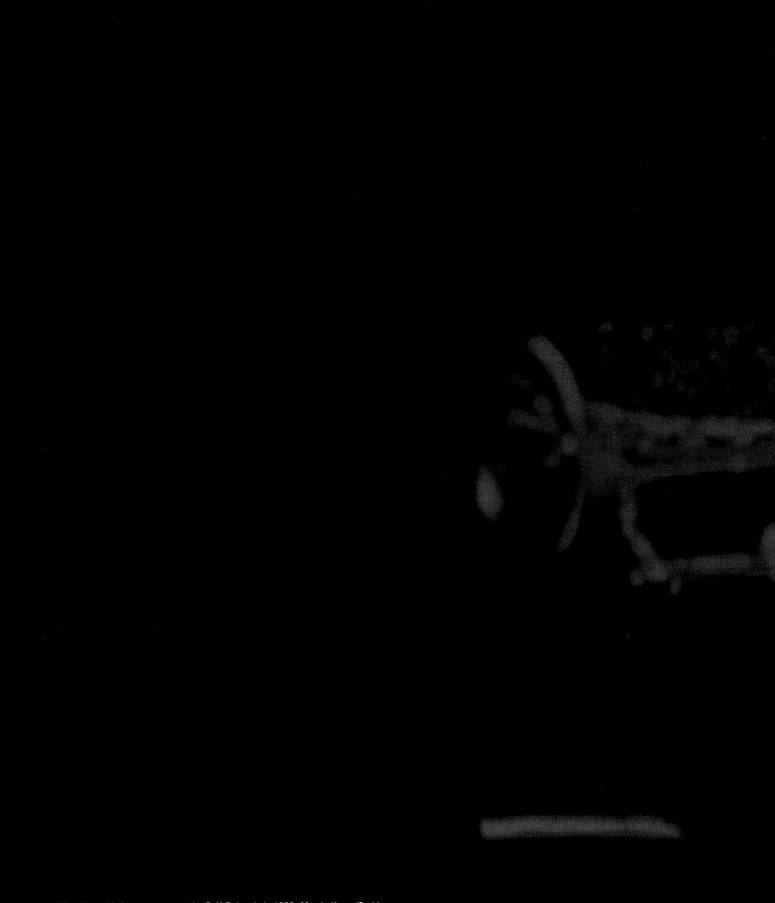

Miles blows his horn on stage at the Café Bohemia in 1956. *Marvin Koner/Corbis*

"Trane was the loudest, fastest saxophonist I've ever heard. He could play real fast and real loud at the same and that's very difficult to do. . . . But Trane could do it and he was phenomenal. I was like he was possessed when he put that horn in his mouth. He was so passionate—fierce—and yet so quiet and gentle when he was playing."

—Miles Davis, *Miles: The Autobiography*, **1989**

OPPOSITE: Flanked by saxophonist John Coltrane, Miles performs at Café Bohemia. *Marvin Koner/Corbis*

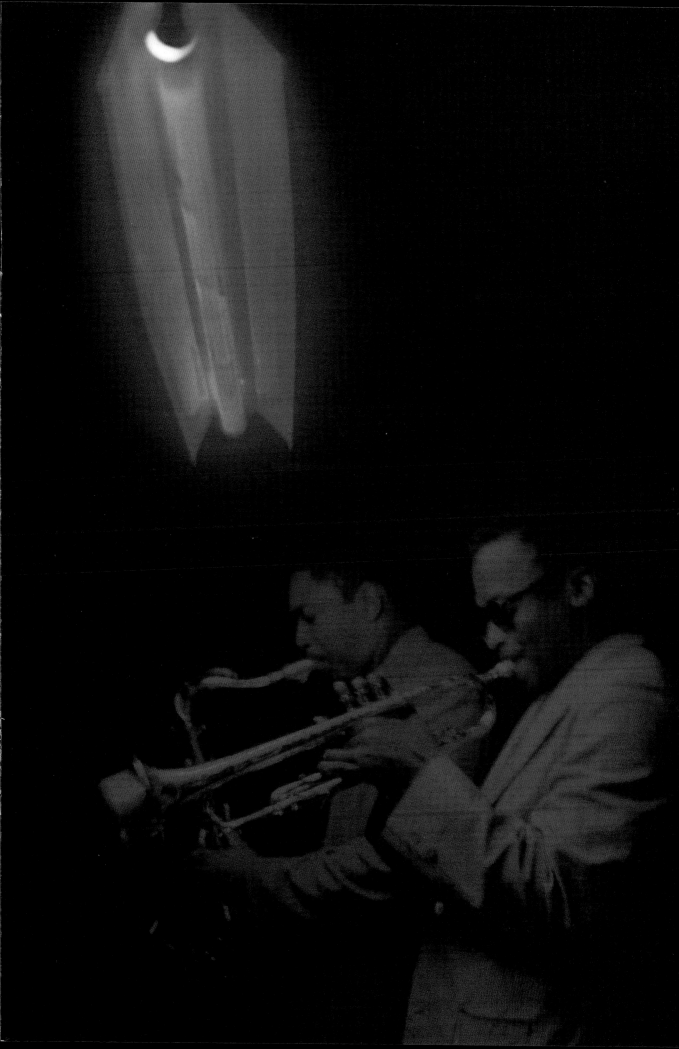

MILES IN FRANCE

by VINCENT BESSIÈRES

Jazz writer **VINCENT BESSIÈRES** was the curator of the exhibit *We Want Miles*. Organized by La Cité de la Musique in Paris, the exhibit subsequently traveled around the globe.

Was it a matter of smell?

Thinking back in his autobiography to the first trip he ever made to Paris, Miles made an odd comment about how smells were different in the City of Light. "It's kind of like coconut and lime in rum all-mixed together. Almost tropical."

Tropical? Did he mean "exotic?"

For a twenty-two-year-old Miles Davis (he turned twenty-three while in France) who had not been out of his country yet, Paris was surely something else, an entirely other world that he discovered with the same excitement as an explorer setting foot into a new land. In France, despite not being able to speak a word, Miles could live another life from what he had experienced until then, growing up in East St. Louis, Illinois, and trying to make a living playing jazz in the nightclubs of New York City. France revealed to Miles another side of living he could not envision until he traveled out of the United States.

Paris made Miles a different man. In 1949, he was constantly smiling. Photographers caught him in the cellars of Saint-Germain-des-Prés hanging out with Bird and French writer Boris Vian, joking at the bar of the Salle Pleyel concert hall with trumpet buddies Kenny Dorham and Oran "Hot Lips" Page, playing around with Juliette Gréco. Miles is all smiles, showing a face that had rarely been seen elsewhere. And would rarely be seen again.

Miles Davis was not the first African American artist to find in Paris a host that would allow him to be different. From Josephine Baker to Langston Hughes, Sidney Bechet to Palmer Hayden, France was a land of promised freedom, even if the way most French people would look at them as "Nègres" was often ambiguous. Some African Americans came to France with great expectations and dreams, others just because there was work. Miles came as the Artist, and he was greeted as such. This made a difference. Expectations were high. And he would fulfill them.

Miles came as the Modern. In the dispute between the moldy figs and the sour grapes, he was clearly an ace on the side of the innovative, of the new sounds. He was brought to Paris as living proof. To make the music of modern times heard live in a city that was still recovering from years of darkness and starvation under the Nazi Occupation. In a country hoping for novelty and lightness, looking for hope and dreams, Miles was the new breed, the sound of the jazz to come. And his trumpet indeed sounded different.

Some happy few had dug his records and Miles' style was already an enigma. French critic André Hodeir dubbed him "elusive" even before he arrived. Charlie Parker was also on the bill, yet he was already a legend. Miles was the new breed, the one who could break new ground. He had already done exactly this a couple of weeks before landing in Paris, by leading and recording in New York his Nonet in sessions that would later be billed as *Birth of the Cool*. The right man at the right place, Miles became part of the myth of the Left Bank spirit, a crowd in which artists of all kinds, intellectuals and merrymakers, were willing to fulfill their life with a complete freedom of thought and acting after suffering from the deprivation of the war years. He was the Black, the American, the Jazz Musician, and his love story with Juliette Gréco provided the idealized picture of a love in black and white to those who were expecting new times.

Miles did not come to Paris because of the lack of jobs in the United States, as so many of his elderly peers had done before the war or would continue to do throughout the next decades. What also made a big difference was his decision not to remain in Paris, as others—drummer Kenny Clarke, saxophonist James Moody, and pianist Bud Powell among them—would soon be doing. France could make Miles smile, allowing him to experience love, friendship, freedom, and pleasure—and to find the energy to go back to where he believed he had to live and create, home. To Miles, France was a shelter, a place he could expect a lot, where things would be different. Here, only music mattered, not race. He could hire a white piano player—Frenchman René Urtreger—and be friends with him, and nobody cared—they were all whites anyway! He could tour with a musician he idolized, such as Lester Young, who epitomized the pre-World War II swing-era, and still be considered as a modern. He could also be challenged in unexpected new ways, such as being asked to record the soundtrack to a movie of a new kind.

Miles never cared much about the soundtrack he provided to Louis Malle's *Ascenseur pour l'échafaud* because the movie was never big in the United States. According to most of the people who

"Juliette was probably the first woman that I loved as an equal human being. . . . It was April in Paris. Yeah, and I was in love."

—Miles Davis, *Miles: The Autobiography*, 1989

LEFT: Juliette Gréco.

"This was my first trip out of the country [going to Paris in 1949] and it changed the way I looked at things forever. . . . It was the freedom of being in France and being treated like a human being, like someone important. Even the band and the music we played sounded better over there."

—Miles Davis, *Miles: The Autobiography*, 1989

Miles flew to Paris on May 7, 1949, to appear at the Festival International de Jazz at the grand Salle Pleyel, organized by impresario Charles Delaunay.

Ascenseur pour l'échafaud poster, Brussels, 1958.

"I was so depressed coming back to this country [the United States] on the airplane that I couldn't say nothing all the way back. I didn't known that shit was going to hit me like that. I was so depressed when I got back that before I knew it, I had a heroin habit that took me four years to kick and I found myself for the first time out of control and sinking faster than a motherfucker toward death."

—Miles Davis, *Miles: The Autobiography*, 1989

were around him at that time, recording an original soundtrack for the film was no big deal. Playing "Four" up-tempo or "Walkin' " in the right groove on stage at the Olympia was the real challenge. But this recording is probably the one that made him a legend in France. Even today, many people first begin to listen to Miles thanks to this legendary soundtrack—and not only because of the music, the noir atmosphere, the elusive playing, but because of the myth surrounding the recording session.

France has always been fascinated by geniuses, people able to create with seeming effortlessness. Writer Boris Vian told the story on the back of the record of Miles improvising the soundtrack for *Ascenseur pour l'échafaud* in a couple of hours at night, without saying much, playing according to the pictures projected on the screen for him to watch. That story fascinated generations of Miles' French admirers. No contract, no big executives, only Miles and Louis Malle alone in the recording studio, and the shadow of a lover who helped things happen.

This mixture of romance and free minds led Miles to places that were out of sight at home where pressure weighed on his back. Louis Malle's movie became part of the Nouvelle Vague spirit, not only for

his use of natural light and shooting outdoors but also because of the importance and the leeway he gave to Miles' music, which followed actress Jeanne Moreau's plight and desperation. One more time, Miles was the right man at the right place.

This experience likely also opened new doors to Miles. With the *Ascenseur pour l'échafaud* soundtrack, Miles experienced a way of creating music in a new, spontaneous way that he would adopt to produce his best-known album, *Kind of Blue*. And from then on, he would consider the studio not only as place to record but also a haven to compose and elaborate music on the spur of the moment.

As jazzmen say, Miles dug France. But France dug Miles, too. Miles became part of France because his talent soared above the performances he gave: he became part of the family. Like Josephine Baker, Sidney Bechet, Richard Wright, or the Art Ensemble of Chicago, Miles was adopted by French people as a part of their story because of the stamp he put on their culture. And for years to come, Miles' sound remained part of their collective memory—the sound of an era, the freedom of the artist, a living image of cool, the idealized romance between jazz and France.

LOVE FOR SALE

by ROBIN D. G. KELLEY

ROBIN D. G. KELLEY is the author of the landmark biography *Thelonious Monk: The Life and Times of an American Original* as well as other titles on jazz and race relations. Before becoming professor of American Studies and Ethnicity at the University of Southern California, he served on the faculty at Columbia University's Center for Jazz Studies.

"Evil genius." "Prince of Darkness." "Endearing with his music, offending with his personality."

For more than half a century, critics have come up with all sorts of phrases to describe the darkness and light that is Miles Davis. Miles commanded attention from every generation since the early days of the Cold War, fostering undying devotion and disgust along the way. Even in death he remains one of the most revered and reviled artists on the planet. Miles is everywhere, the subject of books, new musical interpretations, and a flood of boxed sets and previously unreleased recordings. The posthumous reassessments echo earlier commentary: he is hailed as a musical genius and praised for the beauty and sensitivity of his playing while simultaneously criticized for his brutal treatment of women, his rude and exploitative behavior, his anger toward whites, or for selling out to the forces of pop music. Meanwhile, those really mad at Miles boycott his records.

Most of us cannot reconcile these two sides of Miles because we want our heroes to be likeable, especially when it comes to "America's classical music." But by dividing Miles this way, we miss how the things we don't like about the man are fundamental to what we love about his music. His deep distrust of others, his desire for easy living, his detachment, and his violence derive from the same playa principles behind his romanticism, his coolness and sense of style. Miles' sense of detachment and romanticism might be viewed as part of a singular set of performative practices rooted in a unique aspect of African American urban culture—the hustler's code. The pimp aesthetic.

Now hold on. I'm not calling Miles a pimp, as Stanley Crouch once accused him for going pop. And while Miles confessed to actual pimping during his heroin daze, I'm not suggesting that he needed to be a real pimp to embrace the life. Rather, he was the product of a masculine culture that aspired to be *like* a pimp or a hustler. One thinks immediately of Railroad Bill or Stagolee, or the more contemporary real-life figure of Iceberg Slim. Pimps in African American culture/folklore are more than violent exploiters of women. To this day, they are celebrated as masters of a style, from the language and the stroll, to the clothes, the wheels, and the entourage.

As a youth in East St. Louis, Miles emulated black musicians whose sense of style differed little from the playas, the macks, the hustlers who occupied the same nightclub universe. "I'd sit there and look at them, watch the way they walked and talked, how they fixed their hair, how they'd drink, and of course how they played." He learned well, appearing on more best-dressed lists than any other jazz musician in history. And he knew how to wear his threads—from the tailor-made charcoal gray pinstripe suit, the bright red bell bottoms and the maroon and orange scarf he sported during his funk period, to his long jeri curl and pre-MC Hammer parachute pants of the 1980s—the latter perhaps more pimpish than any of his previous attire.

Even in crisis Miles was camera-ready. In August of 1959 he made front-page news after police officers beat and arrested him while standing in front of Birdland. A photographer captured a cool but indignant Miles sporting his blood-stained white khaki jacket like a badge as he was being carted off by police.

Anyone who has called him a poor showman for walking off stage or turning his back on the audience was not paying attention. Film footage from a 1967 Stockholm concert showcases his mastery of movement. Every gesture seems choreographed but effortless, the way he nonchalantly walks on stage, rubs just behind his ear, places his impeccably manicured fingers to his lips just before bringing the horn to his mouth. His smooth brown skin never breaks a sweat. Even the way he ambles off stage resembles what the kids I grew up with in Harlem used to call a "pimp stroll." Again, the term was never meant as a description of an actual pimp's gait but rather the urban folk image of pimp-like masculinity.

Miles plays his trumpet one-handed during a recording session for Cannonball Adderly's *Somethin' Else* album on March 9, 1958. *Francis Wolff/Mosaic Images/Corbis*

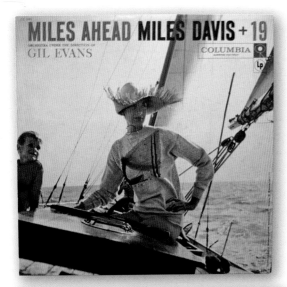

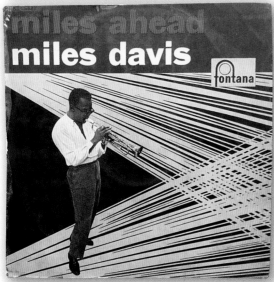

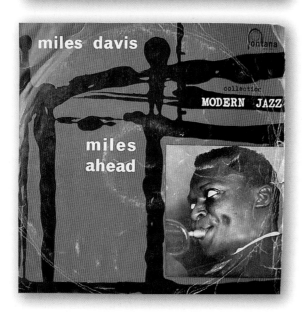

Miles also had a hustler's voice—the voice poet Amiri Baraka once described as his "hipster foghorn bass . . . somewhat mysterious with a touch of street toughness." Miles spoke like he played, embracing the principle that less is more, and became one of the trumpet's greatest storytellers, his use of smears and bent notes giving his playing a distinctively vocal quality. Miles created complete statements with a beginning, middle, and an end: stories that possessed a sense of drama. The more colorful hustlers have been known for their story-telling ability, a source of black oral poetry known as "toasting." Toasts, like sermons, are judged by delivery, phrasing, pacing, and a sense of dynamics that often includes the use of falsetto, whispering, and artfully placed pauses to elicit call and response with the audience.

Miles displayed all of these qualities in his playing. And in typical mack fashion, he would tease us, withholding obvious notes and a musical climax with wonderful cadences tagged at the end of such songs as "If I Were A Bell" or "Bye Bye Blackbird." As tenor saxophonist Benny Golson said of Miles, "He leaves me, always, wanting to hear more."

As much as we hate to admit it, romance is a form of emotional power that could be used to control or oppress. In the 1950s and early 1960s, Miles became famous for romantic ballads. Using his signature Harmon mute, he turned songs of vulnerability into breathtaking stories of seduction. Just listen to "You're My Everything" from *Relaxin' with the Miles Davis Quintet*. He is not pleading here; he is straight mackin', self-assured and full of promises. Beautiful, intelligent women did not flock to Miles in order to be terrorized; he made them believe he loved them.

By the mid-1960s, as the pimp figure began to lose its pride of place in African American urban culture and the new "baadman" characters were the leaders of the black freedom movement, Miles formed his second great quintet with Wayne Shorter, Herbie Hancock, Tony Williams, and Ron Carter. Miles did not lose his storytelling ability, but he became more interested in emancipating musical language and hearing many stories at once. Herbie Hancock called it, " 'controlled freedom' . . . just like a conversation—same thing." Musically at least, the pimp aesthetic was less evident.

Julien "Cannonball" Adderley performs on stage, circa 1958. *Gai Terrell/Redferns/Getty Images*

SOMETHIN'
ELSE
CANNONBALL
ADDERLEY
MILES DAVIS
HANK JONES
SAM JONES
ART BLAKEY
BLUE NOTE 1595

"I did Walkin' for Prestige and man, that album turned my whole life and career around. . . . I wanted to take the music back to the fire and improvisations of bebop, that kind of thing that Diz and Bird had started. But I also wanted to take the music forward into a more funky kind of blues . . . ."

—Miles Davis, *Miles: The Autobiography,* **1989**

With the dawn of the electric Miles in 1969, the Pimp of Darkness came back with a vengeance. In the age when blaxploitation films celebrated the street hustlers and proclaimed funk as *the* urban soundtrack, Miles pushed the aesthetic to the outer limits. On stage, his bright colored threads illuminated by psychedelic lights, his face hidden behind huge dark shades, he looked as if he had just walked off the set of *Superfly.* Miles encouraged multiple conversations but brought back an old-fashioned "call and response" feeling. "Don't finish your phrases," he told his band members. Miles' electric bands sounded like church and the Hustlers Convention all rolled up in one, two sides of the same cultural coin.

As the 1970s came to a close, Miles dropped out of music and descended deeper into cocaine to help him forget his broken body. But just when we thought he was out of the game he rose again. Between his comeback in 1981 and his death ten years later, Miles recorded over a dozen albums and embraced his inner pimp to the point of parody. The opening cut on Miles' 1985 album *You're Under Arrest* is a hilarious audio-verité scene in which police officers from around the world harass Miles, who sits in his car playing the old school gangsta. A year later, he made his acting debut as—what else?—a pimp on *Miami Vice.*

In the end, listening and looking for the pimp aesthetic in Miles ought to make us aware of the pleasures of cool as well as the dark side of romance. We may get nostalgic for the old romantic Miles, for that feeling of being in love, but who understands this better than the mack, that despicable character we find so compelling and attractive? Next time you're on the road digging *Kind of Blue* or *Bitches Brew* and feel the urge to lean to the side and tilt your head back just so, left arm riding the top of the steering wheel, check the rear-view . . . it just might be the pimp in you.

OPPOSITE: Miles plays his trumpet at the New York Jazz Festival in New York City on August 23, 1957. *Bob Parent/Hulton Archive/ Getty Images*

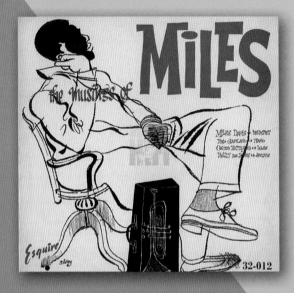

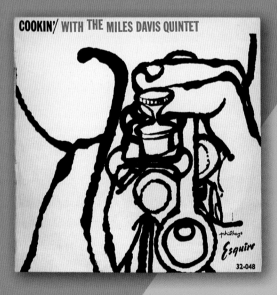

We Proudly Present
DIRECT FROM PARIS, FRANCE
MILES DAVIS
AND HIS BAND
PAULA GREER   All Star Show
CROWN PROPELLER 868 L. 63RD ST.

NOW PLAYING
MILES DAVIS & HIS COMBO
PLUS MARIMACKS Calypso Dance Team
First time in Chicago KALOH Exotic Dancer
The Incredible BILLY GAMBLE, M.C. Singing, Dancing, Comedy
AT CHICAGO'S
BIRDLAND
(formerly Beige Room)
6412 S. Cottage Gr. MU. 4-4400

MILES DAVIS
And His QUARTETTE
Featuring
SONNY ROLLINS
ON TENOR SAX
Sunday Mat. 5-8
MA. 3-9650°
Club Tijuana
"BALTIMORE'S HOUSE OF MODERN JAZZ"
2674 PENNSYLVANIA AVE
Opening Tues., June 28, ART BLAKEY QUINTET

FINAL WEEK
JERI SOUTHERN
MILES DAVIS ALL STARS
TERRY GIBBS QUARTET
BIRDLAND
JAZZ CORNER OF THE WORLD
BROADWAY AT 52ND ST.
JU 6-1368

OPENING TUESDAY NITE!
ONE WEEK ONLY
IN PERSON
MILES DAVIS QUINTET
2 AFTERNOON SESSIONS
SAT. & SUN., 5 to 8 P.M.
COMEDY CLUB
1414 PENNA. AVE., BALTO., MD.

Bob Reisner presents
THE GREATEST IN MODERN JAZZ
MILES DAVIS
TRUMPET
HORACE SILVER—Piano
KENNY CLARKE—Drums
PERCY HEATH—Bass
SUNDAY, JUNE 13
9.00 P. M. to 1 A. M.
OPEN DOOR
55 WEST 3rd STREET

FINAL WEEK
JERI SOUTHERN
MILES DAVIS ALL STARS
TERRY GIBBS QUARTET
BIRDLAND
JAZZ CORNER OF THE WORLD
BROADWAY AT 52ND ST.
JU 6-1368

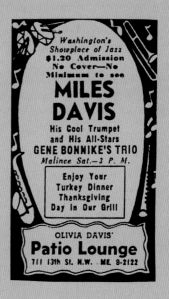

Washington's Showplace of Jazz
$1.20 Admission
No Cover—No Minimum to see
MILES DAVIS
His Cool Trumpet and His All-Stars
GENE BONNIKE'S TRIO
Matinee Sat.—3 P. M.
Enjoy Your Turkey Dinner Thanksgiving Day In Our Grill
OLIVIA DAVIS'
Patio Lounge
711 13th St. N.W. ME. 8-2122

AIR CONDITIONED
THE L. & P. TRIO
PLUS GLORIA SMITH
LITTLE MISS MUFFET ★ DIRECT FROM BIRDLAND
OPENING TUES. OCT. 4
LAST 2 DAYS
MILES DAVIS
AND HIS OWN QUARTET
SUNDAY MATINEE STARTS 6 P.M. TILL 7
CLUB LAS VEGAS
128 WARWICK AVE. AT LEXINGTON ST.
GI. 5-9565

BIRDLAND = the most in jazz in '59

DAKOTA STATON
SHAHIB SHEHAB QUARTET
"WILD BILL" DAVIS TRIO
MAR. 5th thru MAR. 18

MAYNARD FERGUSON and his Orch.
CHICO HAMILTON QUINTET
MAR. 19 thru APR. 1

BUDDY RICH and his 15 pc. Orch.
ART BLAKEY and the JAZZ MESSENGERS
APRIL 2 thru APR. 15

MILES DAVIS SEXTETTE
GIL EVANS and his Band
APR. 16 thru APR. 29

SARAH VAUGHAN
HARRY "SWEETS" EDISON
Johnny SMITH TRIO
APR. 30 thru MAY 20

MAYNARD FERGUSON and his ORCHESTRA
JUNE 4 thru JUNE 17

COUNT Basie AND HIS ORCHESTRA with JOE WILLIAMS
MAY 21 thru JUNE 3

stan KENTON and his ORCH.
JUNE 18 thru JULY 1

ALL STAR JAM SESSION EVERY MONDAY NIGHT

94

4

Kind of
Blue

ON NEW YEAR'S DAY 1958, Miles Davis rang John Coltrane and asked the saxophonist to rejoin his Sextet. Coltrane had been playing with pianist Thelonious Monk—Monk having invited Coltrane to join his band after witnessing Miles punching the much bigger (if much gentler) man backstage at Birdland. While the pairing of two formidable modernists such as Monk and Coltrane had attracted plenty of attention from New York jazz fans, it hadn't proved a great success, with Coltrane struggling with Monk's often obscure melodies. Coltrane immediately agreed to rejoin, and Miles looked forward to playing with the man they nicknamed 'Trane, aware that the saxophonist had overcome his drug and alcohol addictions and now saw music as a spiritual quest.

Miles then convinced Cannonball Adderley to join the Sextet. Adderley played alto saxophone with great skill and warmth, his fat, soulful tone contrasting with Trane's more astringent sound. Adderley had no substance abuse problems, while both pianist Red Garland and bassist Paul Chambers had embraced moderation since they last played with Miles. Drummer Philly Joe Jones remained a problematic junkie, but as Miles rated him as his favorite drummer, he got his job back.

Handbill, Birdland, New York City, 1959.

Entering the studio in February 1958, the Sextet recorded a selection of familiar material, cutting only one new tune, "Milestones" (or "Miles" as it was mistakenly called on the initial LP—and, unbelievably, on the CD reissue). While Davis had previously recorded a tune called "Milestones" for Prestige, this new composition found him exploring modalism for the first time. Pianist and composer George Russell, another habitué of Gil Evans' 55th Street apartment sessions, had long been inspired by a remark Miles had made to him about "wanting to learn all the changes" to codify the modal approach to harmony so as to create a new and broader way to relate to chords. What Russell attempted—with pianist Bill Evans (no relation to Gil)—on his 1957 album *Jazz Workshop* and in his writings now galvanized Miles to attempt the modal approach. On *Milestones*' title track, the Sextet embraced this challenging approach to playing jazz. The modal approach essentially involved the sextet creating solos out of harmony rather than chords, thus further opening the possibilities of what a gifted musician might be able to play. It also created a slower, more deliberate pace, something Davis was interested in exploring.

On *Milestones*' five other selections, they continued to mine the muscular blues that had informed the quintet's Prestige recordings. Tracks like "Sid's Ahead" and "Two Bass Hit" allowed the sextet to stretch out, their superb ensemble playing matched by remarkable soloing. "Straight No Chaser," one of Thelonious Monk's most famous compositions, closes the album and would remain a staple in Davis' set for many years to come. Coltrane, fresh from six months of playing with Monk, takes solos that go off to strange places, stretch way out, yet never lose dynamic.

Tensions between Red Garland and Miles meant a new pianist was needed. Davis approached Bill Evans, a very different player. Evans was white, classically educated and, like Coltrane, a deep thinker who read widely. Miles appreciated Evans' musical ability, and they often spent time together discussing music, with Evans increasing Davis' appreciation of such European classical composers as Ravel and Brahms. Being the only white musician in a band who represented a very black aesthetic meant Evans encountered some hostility from black audiences (while Miles was never subtle when it came to comments concerning race). But as a unit the sextet performed superbly. Bill Evans only lasted eight months with the Sextet—a combination of events, including a dislike of the road warrior lifestyle, made him leave. Replaced by Wynton Kelly, a pianist of West Indian origin whose playing came from a very different place, the Sextet continued playing to adoring audiences.

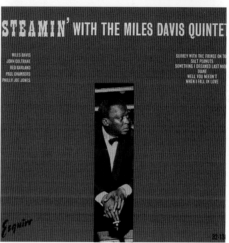

Poster, Jazz For Civil Rights, Hunter College Auditorium, New York City, October 4, 1959.

Making his televised debut, Miles leads the Miles Davis Orchestra on CBS television's "Theater for a Story" on April 2, 1959. *CBS via Getty Images*

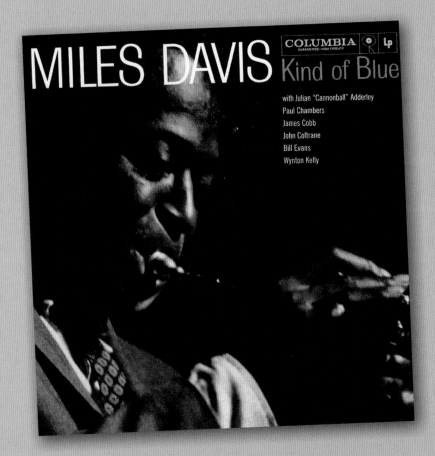

with Julian "Cannonball" Adderley
Paul Chambers
James Cobb
John Coltrane
Bill Evans
Wynton Kelly

"I didn't write out the music for Kind of Blue, *but brought in sketches for what everybody was supposed to play because I wanted a lot of spontaneity in the playing . . . ."*

—Miles Davis, *Miles: The Autobiography*, 1989

*"*Kind of Blue *also came out of the modal thing I started on* Milestones. *This time I added some other kind of sound I remembered from being back in Arkansas, when we were walking home from church and they were playing these bad gospels. So that kind of feeling came back to me and I started remembering what that music sounded like and felt like. That feeling is what I was trying to get close to. That feeling had got in my creative blood, my imagination, and I had forgotten it was there. I wrote this blues that tried to get back to that feeling I had when I was six years old, walking with my cousin along that Arkansas road."*

—Miles Davis, *Miles: The Autobiography*, 1989

OPPOSITE: Miles sits pensively with his trumpet during a studio session, October 1959. *Hulton Archive/Getty Images*

KIND OF BLUE 1958—1963 • 99

Miles is booked by New York City police on August 25, 1959, following a fracas with patrolman Gerald Kilduff. The officer ordered Miles to move along from sidewalk outside Birdland, where Miles was getting some fresh air between sets. Davis was hit on the head with a blackjack and arrested. Charged with assault and disorderly conduct, Davis was released on $525 bail from Felony Court.
Hal Mathewson/NY Daily News via Getty Images

OPPOSITE: Miles records at 30th Street Studios in New York City, in 1959.
Michael Ochs Archives/Getty Images

Advertising Flyer, Broadcast Music Inc. (BMI), 1961.

Columbia suggested Miles and Gil Evans record George Gershwin's "folk opera" *Porgy and Bess* and, after some deliberation, Davis agreed. Evans wrote a score that utilized elements of Gershwin's compositions while reshaping the music as abstract jazz. Well received by critics and the public, *Porgy and Bess* kept Miles in fine suits and fast cars (and he now generously supported the three children he had fathered with Irene).

Yet Miles' mind was focused on modal jazz and night after night he made the band listen to tapes of their live performances while he directed them toward a sound he heard in his head. Before they could all come together, Philly Joe Jones had to go—his heroin addiction making him unreliable. Drummer Jimmy Cobb replaced Jones, and Miles worked toward what he believed would be his "crossover record" based on ideas he and Bill Evans had discussed. To do so Miles invited Bill Evans to rejoin the Sextet for the March 2, 1959, recording date at Columbia's New York studio on 30th Street. Irving Townsend is listed as producer although he did little more than oversee the sessions while Miles directed the musicians. Engineer Fred Plout, whose placement of microphones and expert ears helped determine the perfect take, played an important role.

When Wynton Kelly arrived at the studio he was annoyed to see Bill Evans there. Miles informed Kelly that he would be needed only for one tune, "Freddie Freeloader": as this was a blues, Miles felt Wynton's playing was more suitable to it than Bill's. Thus "Freddie Freeloader"—named after a Philadelphia bartender and Miles' gofer—was the first tune the sextet cut. This twelve-bar B-flat blues is simplicity itself, the two-note motifs allowing Kelly to solo with great rhythmic flourish before Davis, Coltrane, and then Adderley all take turns stretching out with magnificent solos before returning to the theme. Everyone involved knew something special was underway, and it must have seemed odd for Kelly to give up the piano stool, but Bill Evans had been shaping the material with Miles and wanted to get to work.

OPPOSITE: Miles, circa 1960. *AF Archive/Alamy*

Miles and John Coltrane perform at the Sutherland Hotel Lounge in Chicago, Illinois, on February 21, 1960. Around the time of this show, Trane gave notice to Miles that he would be leaving to start his own band. *Ted Williams/Michael Ochs Archives/Getty Images*

Poster, Shelly's Manne-Hole,
Hollywood, California,
April 5–14, 1963.

"So What" was the first number they recorded. This nine-minute recording has since gone on to be Miles Davis' most famous number, its simple rhythmic hook, unforgettable melody, and sublime beauty marking it as one of the most striking pieces of music ever recorded. Richard Cook wrote of "So What," "The mystery of the piece is its air of elusive, almost secretive possibility. One feels that the solos could go anywhere, could follow any path, could drift on without stopping, and not feel 'wrong.' It is a defining piece of jazz, if one identifies that music as something played by intuition and living on its instincts. For once, there seems to be no contrast in the solos played by Davis, Coltrane, and Adderley: they move seamlessly together, as if each man were playing his part in a predetermined plan."

The sextet then recorded "Blue In Green," a funereal-paced meditation for Evans and Davis to improvise upon. Coltrane takes a brief solo, but this haunting number is largely a dialogue between piano and muted trumpet. Miles had intended to record a fourth number that day yet they ran out of time, instead reassembling on April 22. Here they began with "Flamenco Sketches," a drifting, Spanish-flavored piece that with a plaintive air. The four soloists again pursue a quiet, contemplative expressiveness, one tender and intimate, while Chambers and Cobb perfectly map out a quiet pulse.

"All Blues" was the final recording and at 11 minutes 33 seconds, the longest. It features a catchy three-note figure, and the ensemble take their time to glide through, Evans' piano vamping before each of the horns takes a solo, with Coltrane providing the most shimmering solo of his career. As "All Blues" faded out, Miles Davis knew he had a finished album.

Kind of Blue, named by Miles as he felt it fitted the album's mood, was released on August 19, 1959. It proved an instant hit, garnering rave reviews across a wide variety of publications and heavy radio play on jazz stations. Jazz fans were immediately in awe of the album and have remained so ever since, *Kind of Blue* quickly becoming the best-selling serious jazz album ever. This quietly perfect album offers an expert balance between six gifted musicians at their creative peak. The translucent feel of the music—its mystique and elegance—has often been copied but never equaled, and Miles' golden trumpet tone (especially his solo on "So What") is one of startling beauty.

Kind of Blue finds Miles at his most contemplative. Happy with his personal life—the beautiful actress Frances Taylor had moved into his Manhattan apartment—his success and music, wealth and health, Miles had gone about creating an extremely lyrical and tender masterpiece. Or perhaps that should be "co-creating," as Bill Evans would later claim that he wrote "Blue In Green" and co-wrote "Flamenco Sketches," and several people close to the sessions believe Gil Evans may have contributed the opening melody for "So What." Miles claimed sole publishing of the five tunes (and thus never had to share the fortune the album earned—his five bandmates were paid union scale) but would admit that Bill Evans contributed much to the album's overall sound and feel. Miles may have been mean when it came to sharing *Kind of Blue*'s income but no one ever questioned that the album was the result of his remarkable vision. Indeed, so full of creative fire was the trumpeter that in a twelve-month period he had recorded the music of *Milestones*, *Porgy and Bess*, and *Kind of Blue*.

Kind of Blue's success continues to this day—on October 8, 2008, the Recording Industry Association Of North America certified it quadruple platinum status for sales of more than four million copies in the United States alone. Its influence can be found in many different areas of music: From Duane Allman claiming he modeled the Allman Brothers' jazzy blues jams on the album's horn interplay, to contemporary classical composers Steve Reich and Terry Riley stating that they based their minimalist aesthetic on *Kind of Blue*'s perfect surface, to today's DJ re-mixers who aim for a similar mix of stealth, dynamic, and atmosphere in their computer-generated sounds. *Kind of Blue* pervades the art of music making. As it should be. Miles stated that a major influence on the music he wrote for *Kind of Blue* involved witnessing a dance and music troupe from the West African state of Guinea, while "Flamenco Sketches" hinted at his love for Latin music.

But not everything went smoothly. Stepping outside Birdland on the evening of August 26, 1959, Miles became involved in a fracas with New York police that led to him being beaten and arrested. The incident—witnessed by many—brought about international newspaper headlines with the front cover of Britain's *Melody Maker* bearing a photo of the bleeding trumpeter and the headline "This Is What They Did To Miles."

Davis took the Sextet on the road for an extended tour to capitalize on *Kind of Blue*'s success with Trane finally leaving while on the West Coast.

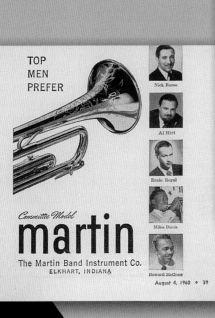

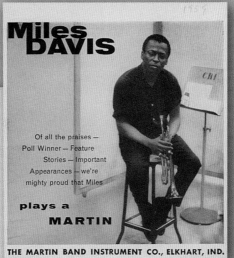

As Miles' fame grew, trumpet makers vied for his endorsement on their wares as a route to selling horns to players.

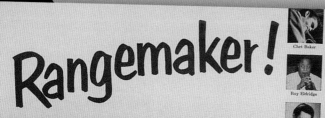

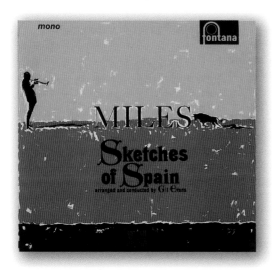

Columbia, wanting to capitalize on *Kind of Blue*'s soaring sales success, suggested Davis and Gil Evans again join forces. The two friends agreed, and chose to explore Spanish music, which mirrored the then-current American craze for all things Iberian, including Ernest Hemmingway's tales of bullfighting as well as flamenco music and dance troupes. Saxophonist Art Pepper once noted, "Gil's understanding of Miles was perfect," and the two men shared a deep friendship and musical bond. Evans first arranged Joaquin Rodrigo's "Concierto de Aranjuez" alongside Spanish folk and classical compositions. Recording on November 20, 1959, and March 10, 1960, Paul Chambers and Jimmy Cobb and lead trombonist Frank Rehak (from *Miles Ahead* and *Porgy and Bess*) all played on the sessions alongside some two dozen classical and jazz players. Recording sessions proved difficult for all involved: The classical players lacking the improvisation skills Evans demanded, while the jazz players found the arrangements impossibly difficult. Teo Macero, a new Columbia employee who would go on to work as producer with Miles for the next fifteen years, had to get permission to extend the budget. Davis took a ten-minute trumpet solo on "Solea," perhaps the longest yet recorded, and across *Sketches of Spain* his playing is often remarkable. Yet the album—which proved an instant hit, selling more than 120,000 copies in the United States—is an often rather forced mix of classical, flamenco, and jazz.

"That was the hardest thing for me to do on Sketches of Spain*: to play the parts on the trumpet where someone was supposed to be singing, especially when it was ad-libbed, like most of the time. The difficulty came when I tried to do parts that were in between the words and stuff when the singer is singing. Because you've got all those Arabic musical scales up in there, black African scales that you can hear. And they modulate and bend and twist and snake and move around."*

—Miles Davis, *Miles: The Autobiography*, 1989

"I got this album, Someday My Prince Will Come, and you know who's on the jacket cover? My wife—Frances [Taylor]. I just got to thinking that as many record albums as Negroes buy, I hadn't ever seen a Negro girl on a major album cover unless she was the artist. There wasn't any harm meant—they just automatically thought about a white model and ordered one. It was my album and I'm Frances' prince, so I suggested that they use her for a model, and they did."

—Miles Davis, The *Playboy* Interview, 1962

Hiring Hank Mobley on saxophone, the Quintet began touring, performing more in a hard bop style than *Kind of Blue*'s gentle textures. In March 1961, Miles entered the studio to record *Someday My Prince Will Come*, an album that features guest appearances from Philly Joe Jones and Coltrane, the latter recording with Davis for what would turn out to be the final time. *Someday My Prince Will Come* featured Frances Davis (the couple had married in December 1960) on the cover—a black model appearing on an LP cover was a rare event at the time—and the couple shifted into a converted Manhattan church he had purchased for over $100,000. Miles kept feeling pain in his joints and after seeing a doctor discovered that he suffered from sickle cell anemia. Mixing his medication with heavy drinking and increased cocaine abuse found Miles getting more paranoid and often attacking Frances. In May 1961, Miles played his first Carnegie Hall concert with Gil Evans conducting a twenty-one-piece orchestra. He played brilliantly, although his performance was disrupted by Max Roach taking the stage to protest against the charity Miles was playing the concert to raise funds for.

Columbia insisted that Miles and Gil Evans again record together, and in November 1962 the two friends entered the studio once again. The resulting album, *Quiet Nights*, was an attempt to continue Miles' association with Latin music by cashing in on the bossa nova craze. But things did not go well—Miles was often ill, while Gil did not complete his arrangements. Finally, there was only twenty minutes of finished music, and Columbia had to add an old outtake to make the project releasable. For the first time in many years, critics and the general public were hostile towards Miles' latest effort.

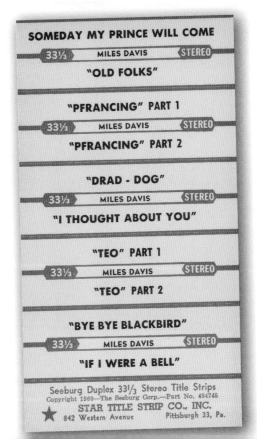

Working again with Gil Evans, Miles recorded the album *Quiet Nights* at 30th Street Studios in New York City in August 1962. *Both images Michael Ochs Archives/ Getty Images*

PURE GENIUS

Devoid of vibrato, spartan in its simplicity, his playing is an artist's eloquent statement about the world in which he lives. One critic called it "deathly in its purity." Another described it as having "the virginal clarity of a Sistine choirboy." Miles himself said: "Don't write about the music. It speaks for itself."

It does. You can hear it in his new album, *Quiet Nights.* Listen to the textured Brazilian rhythms of "Corcovado." Or the sweet, pure sound of his horn on "Wait Till You See Her" and "Once Upon a Summertime." It is pure art.

MILES DAVIS ON COLUMBIA RECORDS

"I wouldn't have no other arranger but Gil Evans— we couldn't be much closer if he was my brother."

—Miles Davis, the *Playboy* interview, 1962

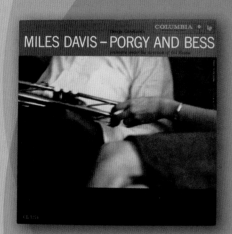

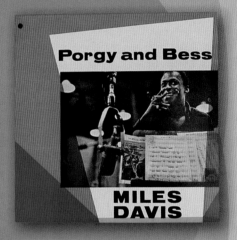

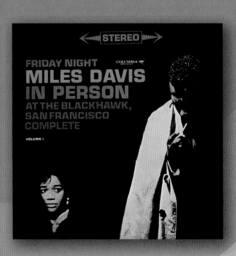

OPPOSITE: Miles performs on stage during a tour of Great Britain in September and October, 1960. *Gai Terrell/Redferns*

MILES, NEWPORT, AND THE BUSINESS OF JAZZ

by GEORGE WEIN

Jazz promoter and producer **GEORGE WEIN** is one of the world's most famous jazz impresarios and the most important non-player in jazz history. He is the founder of the Newport Jazz Festival. In 2005, he was named a "Jazz Master" by the National Endowment for the Arts. He is the author of an autobiography, *Myself Among Others: A Life in Music*.

Early in 1952, Storyville At New Haven, a club I opened for a disastrous few weeks, welcomed a sextet that had been organized by Symphony Sid (Torin). Sid was the voice behind the live radio broadcasts from Birdland. He had worked with Shaw Artists to set up a tour for his bebop all-stars. The group consisted of Jimmy Heath on tenor saxophone, his brother Percy on bass, J. J. Johnson on trombone, Milt Jackson on vibraphone, Kenny Clarke on drums, and Miles Davis on trumpet.

At the beginning of the engagement, Symphony Sid told me not to give Miles any money. I was paying the group $1,200 for the week—from which all of their expenses, including Sid's managerial fee and the agent's percentage, were being extracted. I paid this amount directly to Sid, and he paid the musicians. Miles, who was deep into drugs at this time, probably owed Sid some money from their last gig.

Later that same night, Miles approached me.

"George," he said, "give me ten dollars."

"Sid told me not to give you any money, Miles. I can't do it."

"George," he said, as if he hadn't heard me, "give me five dollars."

"Come on, Miles, I can't do it. The man said not to give you any bread."

"George, give me a dollar."

"Miles—"

"Give me fifty cents, George. Give me a quarter. George, give me a penny."

That was my first conversation with Miles Davis.

Miles pauses during a Jazz At The Philharmonic concert in West Germany during Spring 1960. *Michael Ochs Archives/Getty Images*

In 1955, during a trip to New York City that spring while I was planning the second Newport Jazz Festival, I stopped by the Basin Street East club. Miles Davis was sitting alone at a table in the corner. When Miles had played Storyville At New Haven, he'd been a pain in the ass. We didn't have much of a relationship. But when I walked into the club, he called me over and asked a question.

"Are you having a jazz festival up at Newport this year?"

"Yeah, Miles," I replied.

He looked me in the face and rasped: "You can't have a jazz festival without me."

"Miles," I said, "do you want to come to Newport?"

"You can't have a jazz festival without me," he repeated.

"If you want to be there, I'll call Jack," I said. Jack Whittemore was Miles' agent.

"You can't have a jazz festival without me," he said again. Miles had a way of getting his point across. Although I had already sketched out the program, I knew that I would somehow fit him onto the bill. Miles was in better physical shape in 1955 than he had been in recent years. But he didn't have a working group. The economics of jazz were such that it was difficult for *anyone* to keep a band. Players took whatever work they could get. So I added Miles onto a jam session that already featured Zoot Sims on tenor saxophone, Gerry Mulligan on baritone, and Thelonious Monk on piano. These musicians were all willing to work as individual artists, without their respective groups. Percy Heath and Connie Kay were already scheduled to play earlier in the same program with the Modern Jazz Quartet, so I asked them to serve as the rhythm section.

Because of his late addition to the festival, Davis' name wasn't even printed in our program book. But his presence was felt that night. He overcame the inadequacies of the sound system by putting the microphone right into the bell of his trumpet—and playing Monk's "Round Midnight." The clarity of his sound pierced the air over Newport's Freebody Park like nothing else we heard onstage

Program, Newport Jazz Festival, 1961.

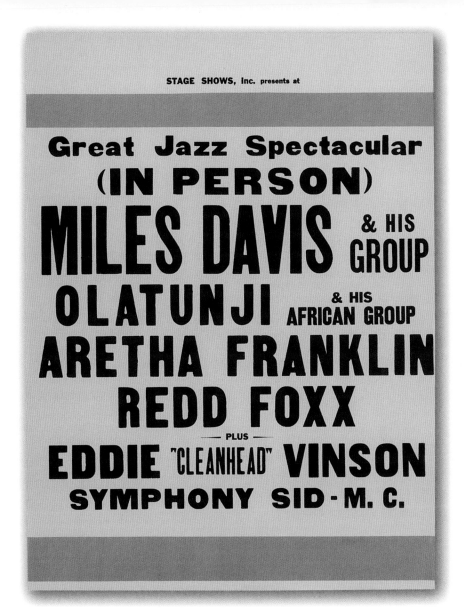

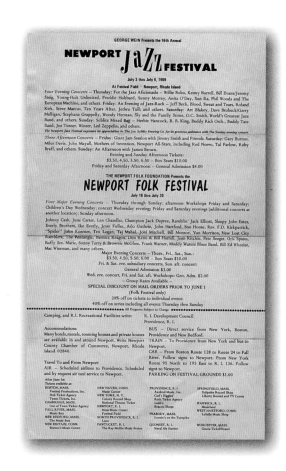

ABOVE: Flyer, Newport Jazz Fest, 1969.

LEFT: Poster, Newport Jazz Festival, 1961.

that year. It was electrifying for the audience out on the grass, the musicians backstage, and the critics—some of whom had opined that Miles' career was already over.

In his autobiography, Miles claims to have played "Round Midnight" with a mute. This was the way he would record it a few years later on 'Round About Midnight for Columbia Records. But he played the ballad with an open horn that night at Newport. My memory is as clear on that point as the sound that rang from the bell of the horn. Bootleg recordings of the jam session, taped from a Voice of America broadcast, confirm my recollection.

A point of interest in these tapes is that Miles does not appear to play well with Monk comping behind him (in "Hackensack"). When Monk lays out, Miles swings easily—"Now's the Time."

Miles also writes about how he had struggled with "Round Midnight" for a long time. Newport marked his victory over the tune. "When I got off the bandstand," he writes, "everybody was looking at me like I was a king or something—people were running up to me

offering me record deals. All the musicians there were treating me like I was a god, and all for a solo that I had had trouble learning a long time ago. It was something else, man, looking out at all those people and then seeing them suddenly standing up and applauding for what I had done."

As Miles descended from the stage, he passed by me. His only words were in the form of a complaint: "Monk plays the wrong changes to 'Round Midnight.'"

I laughed. "Miles, what do you want? He wrote the song!"

Miles Davis had the jazz world in his pocket at that moment, and he knew it. He handled it with characteristic aplomb. But even Miles couldn't ignore the fact that this single performance had energized his entire career. His Newport appearance led to the beginning of what would be a longstanding relationship with Columbia Records. The fact that his comeback took place on the Newport stage helped to validate the festival among the jazz elite. In this way, July 17, 1955, was a good night for both of us.

Miles and his band plays the Antibes Jazz Festival in France, on July 26, 1963.
Pierre Fournier/Sygma/Corbis

OPENING TUESDAY!

Miles Davis
at the
BLACKHAWK

★ ★ ★ ★ ★ ★ ★ ★ ★
Before Going Out Consult
Small's Jazz Calendar
Always A Live Crowd
Always Live Entertainment!
CHRIS COLUMBUS
June 3-15
JAY JAY JOHNSON
June 17-22
MILES DAVIS
June 24-29
JIMMY SMITH
July 1-13
MAX ROACH
July 15-27
HORACE SILVER
July 29-Aug. 10
SONNY ROLLINS
Aug. 12-Aug. 24
Plus Special Attractions
SMALLS' PARADISE
2294 Seventh Avenue at 135th Street, New York City
AUdubon 6-8619 · AUdubon 6-8620
★ ★ ★ ★ ★ ★ ★ ★ ★

MILES DAVIS
BAND
SONNY STITT

TUESDAY NITE — JAZZ CONCERT

PARKING BY UNIFORMED ATTENDANTS

Sutherland Hotel & Lounge
47th and DREXEL BOULEVARD

HARLEM'S HIGH SPOT
APOLLO
One Week Only — Beg. Fri., Oct. 17th

JAZZ   BIRDLAND STYLE

THE DEVINE
SARAH VAUGHAN

MILES DAVIS SEXTET

THE WAILERS | JOHNNY RICHARDS BAND | SID

WEDNESDAY NITE AMATEURS   SATURDAY MIDNITE S

BOB MALTZ presents
Miles - Monk - & Mulligan!

JAZZ
at
TOWN HALL
West 43rd Street   N.Y.C.
FRIDAY, NOVEMBER 28
TWO SHOWS — 8 P.M. and 11 P.M.
— IN PERSON —
MILES DAVIS AND HIS SEXTET
THELONIOUS MONK AND HIS BAND
GERRY MULLIGAN AND HIS GROUP
Extra! **JIMMY GIUFFRE '3'**
Bob Brookmeyer · Jim Hall
$2.00 - $2.85 - $3.85
Mail Order and Box Office Now!

● at TOWN HALL   113 W. 43rd Street
Friday, Nov. 28, 8 p.m. and 11 p.m.
MILES DAVIS and his sextet with Cannonball Adderly
and John Coltrane
THELONIOUS MONK and his band.
GERRY MULLIGAN and his quartet.
EXTRA! The JIMMY GIUFFRE "3" featuring Bob
Brookmeyer and Jim Hall
Tickets $3.85 2.85 2.00 by mail or at box office
BEST SEATS AVAILABLE NOW!

JAZZ AT THE HOWARD

NOW THRU THURSDAY, DEC. 18 — CONTINUOUS
PERFORMANCE — MIDNITE SHOWS FRIDAY &
SATURDAY, DEC. 12-13 — RESERVED SEATS —
ORCHESTRA ONLY — FOR BOTH MIDNITES NOW
ON SALE AT BOX OFFICE AND SUPER MUSIC STORES.

MILES DAVIS
and HIS SEXTET with
"CANNONBALL" ADDERLY
JOHN COLETRANE
"RED" GARLAND
"PHILLY" JOE JONES

BRILLIANT PIANIST
★ **HORACE SILVER** QUINTET

AT THE ORGAN
★ **JIMMY SMITH** TRIO

"SENOR" BLUES"
★ **BILL HENDERSON**

SONGSTRESS OF NOTE
★ **BETTY CARTER**

NEWPORT JAZZ FESTIVAL STARS
★ **THE JAZZ DANCERS**

MASTERS OF CEREMONIES
★ WMAL'S FELIX GRANT
★ WOOK'S AL "Mr. Jazz" JEFFERSON

HARLEM'S HIGH SPOT
APOLLO
ONE WEEK ONLY — BEG. FRIDAY, MAR. 13th

Miles DAVIS SEXTETTE
FROM BLUES TO JAZZ
Ruth BROWN
AT LONG LAST RETURNED
Thelonious MONK

JOHNNY RICHARDS Band

WED NITE AMATEURS   :   SAT. MIDNITE SHOW

NOW - ALL THIS WEEK - THE TITANS OF AMERICAN JAZZ

MILES DAVIS SEXTET
☆ MILES DAVIS · TRUMPET
☆ CANNONBALL ADDERLEY · ALTO SAX
☆ PAUL CHAMBERS · BASS ☆ RED GARLAND · PIANO
☆ JOHN COLTRAINE · TENOR SAX
☆ PHILLY JO JONES · DRUMS

FORTY MINUTE
SETS EVERY HOUR

PGH'S LEADING DOWNTOWN NITE CLUB
Lenny Litman's **COPA**
818 LIBERTY AVE. · CO. 1-4200

NEXT WEEK
THE PLAYMATES
"JO ANN"

THE VILLAGE VOICE PRESENTS

JAZZ
with JEAN SHEPHERD
SAT., APRIL 5 (Two Sensational Shows)   8.30 and 11.15 p. m.
at TOWN HALL, 113 West 43rd St.
FEATURING THE TWO TITANS OF THE TRUMPET!
DIZZY GILLESPIE   MILES DAVIS
PLUS THESE MASTERS OF MODERN JAZZ!
STAN GETZ   J.J. JOHNSON
SONNY STITT   DON ELLIOTT
OSCAR PETTIFORD   CANNONBALL ADDERLEY
PHILLY JOE JONES   PAUL CHAMBERS
OSIE JOHNSON   JOHN COLTRANE
AND MANY OTHERS
Tickets $2, $2.50, $3. (Best Seats Available Now!) Box Office and Mail Order. Also at Village Voice Office

---

JAZZ LTD.
MILES DAVIS
CANNON BALL ADDERLEY — RED GARLAND
JOHN COLTRANE — PAUL CHAMBERS — JIMMY COBB
TONITE | SPOTLIT
9 'TIL 3 A.M. | 13th & Rhode Island Ave.

Cafe Bohemia

"The most adventurous jazz spot in
New York" — Saturday Review
"The foremost of the jazz rooms" —
Robert Sylvester, News

Now thru June 16
ART BLAKEY'S
Jazz Messengers

Now thru July 7
ZOOT SIMS - AL COHN
Quintet

June 17 - 27
The **NEW MILES DAVIS**
Quintet
Featuring Sonny Rollins

June 28 - July 7
"CANNONBALL" ADDERLY
Quintet

CAFE BOHEMIA
15 Barrow Street
Just off Sheridan Square

FOR RESERVATIONS
CH 3-9274

ENJOY A GREAT SHOW IN C-O-O-L COMFORT!
4719 SOUTH PARKWAY
AT S-9585
FREE LIGHTED PARKING
MATINEES

REGAL

STARTS NEXT
FRIDAY, JULY 24th
FOR ONE WEEK ONLY!

ON STAGE 1st Annual Regal
in person JAZZ FESTIVAL
THE GREATEST ARRAY OF JAZZ STARS EVER TO
APPEAR IN A SINGLE STAGE SHOW PRODUCTION!

DAKOTA STATON
America's Dazzling
Queen of Song

MILES DAVIS
And His Terrific
Quintet

SONNY STITT
and His Prestige
Recording
ORCHESTRA

NIPSY RUSSELL
Comedy Sensation
of Broadway and
Hollywood

LEON THOMAS
"Rage of Las Vegas"

JIMMY SMITH
and His Trio

PLUS A GREAT SCREEN ATTRACTIONS

JAZZ
JAZZ LTD.—THE BIGGEST NAMES IN JAZZ
STARTS TONIGHT
MILES DAVIS ALL STARS
AHMAD JAMAL
Starts June 17
SPOTLITE
1300 RHODE ISLAND AVE. N.E.

Opening Tues., Jan. 21
— 6 — BIG NITES — 6 —
MILES DAVIS Sextet
— with —
"Johnny" Coltrane   Paul Chambers
"Cannonball" Adderly   "Red" Garland
"Philly Joe" Jones
"THE JAZZ SPOT OF BROOKLYN"
The Continental
794 NOSTRAND AVE.   BROOKLYN, N.Y.
(bet. Prospect and Park Pl.)

THIS WEEK ONLY!
Nightly thru September 6th
IN PERSON!

MILES DAVIS
QUINTET
Plus THE THREE SOUNDS TRIO

COTTON CLUB
15 N. Illinois Ave., Atlantic City
Res.: ATLANTIC CITY 5-9462

HARLEM'S HIGH SPOT
APOLLO
AIR CONDITIONED
HELD OVER TILL SUNDAY, JULY 31

MILES DAVIS Quintet   Sonny Stitt

Thelonious MONK TRIO

JAMES MOODY BAND

Betty Carter "MOMS" Mabley

WED. NITE AMATEURS   SAT. MIDNITE SHOW

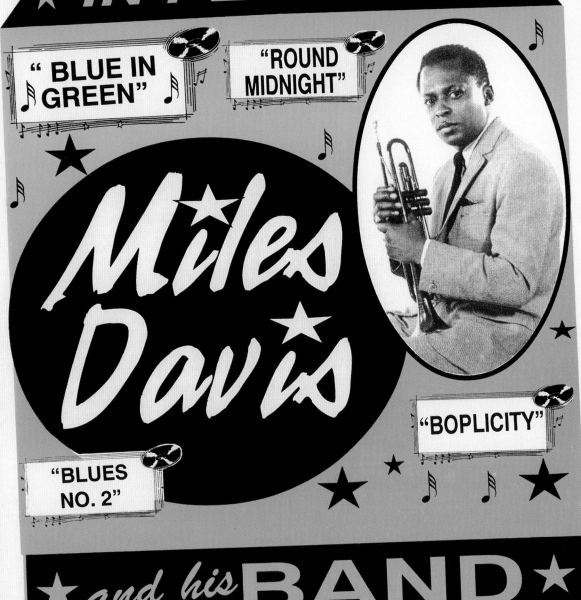

CHAPTER

5

A New Energy

1964–1968

MILES' BEHAVIOR CONTINUED TO BE ERRATIC, and in early 1963 Wynton Kelly and Paul Chambers left to form an acoustic trio while Hank Mobley went off on his own. The implosion of his Quintet cost Miles $25,000 in lost bookings and he hurriedly assembled a new band. John Coltrane recommended a Memphis sax player named George Coleman who had started out touring with bluesman B. B. King and played hard bop with an earthy, soulful tone. Ron Carter, a fluid bassist with strong harmonic knowledge thanks to his classical training, proved more than a fitting replacement for Chambers. Saxophonist Frank Stozier and pianist Harold Mabern were also hired.

After six weeks on the road the Quintet returned to New York and, this time, Jimmy Cobb handed in his notice while Miles fired Mabern and Stozier. Davis put the word out that he was looking for young musicians and got tipped to a seventeen-year-old drummer from Boston named Tony Williams. Miles invited Williams to audition. He then phoned Herbie Hancock, a twenty-three-year-old piano-playing prodigy, and asked him to sit in. For the first two days, as Williams and Hancock rehearsed with Coleman and Carter, Miles listened to the musicians via an intercom. On the third day, with Gil Evans and Philly Joe Jones observing, he joined in the rehearsal but only to play a handful of notes. He then announced that they should arrive at a specified recording studio the next day. This was Miles' manner of telling Williams and Hancock they were in the band. After recording the politely received *Seven Steps to Heaven* album, the new quintet toured Europe to great acclaim.

OPPOSITE: Poster, Famous Ballroom, Baltimore, Maryland, 1960s.

Back in the United States, the quintet recorded the live album, *My Funny Valentine*, at New York's Lincoln Center on February 12, 1964. The concert was ostensibly held to raise funds for voter registration in Mississippi and Louisiana—Civil Rights were by now a dominant issue across the United States, and Miles, while not in the habit of getting involved in political activity, realized that his status as an icon of black artistry and self-determination meant he should lend his weight to the cause. Yet the Quintet's performance almost never happened. Upon arriving at the venue Miles informed his musicians that since this was a charitable event they would not be paid. A rebellion ensured, and Miles had to relent and agree to pay the players. Ironically, the Quintet did not believe they played well—in a tense mood and disliking the Lincoln Center's acoustics, everyone felt aggrieved. Yet on listening back to tapes of their performance the musicians were surprised by the music's beauty.

Teo Macero had recorded the concert with the hope of releasing it. So pleased was he with the quintet's performance he divided the recordings into two separate albums: the first, *My Funny Valentine*, would contain the slow and medium-tempo numbers, while the second, *Four & More*, consisted of more uptempo material.

Issued in May 1965, *My Funny Valentine*'s cover photo found Miles wearing a dapper jacket and tie and cradling his trumpet while looking unsettled. It is one of the classic portraits of the trumpeter. The title track, written by Rodgers and Hart in 1937, had long been a jazz standard with the likes of Frank Sinatra and Chet Baker having crooned "Valentine," and it got a beautifully mournful treatment by Miles. The album sold strongly and remains one of the great live jazz albums. Ian Carr wrote of the live recording, "The playing throughout the album is inspired, and Miles in particular reaches tremendous heights. Anyone who wanted to get a vivid idea of the trumpeter's development over the previous eight years or so should compare [earlier recordings of "My Funny Valentine" and "Stella by Starlight"] with the versions on this 1964 live recording."

If the Quintet were sounding fabulous, there were many unhappy scenes offstage. By now Miles had gotten into a habit of not always turning up for concerts, something that George Coleman found extremely stressful. To add to the stress, Coleman himself was ostracized by Tony Williams. The teenage drummer's leanings towards free jazz as recently pioneered by saxophonist Ornette Coleman were helping shape the Quintet's new sound, and Coleman recalled Williams describing him as "not hip enough." Miles sided with Williams, and Coleman, unhappy with this and the trumpeter's capricious behavior, announced he would not be joining the Quintet for their tour of Japan that summer. At Williams' insistence, Miles employed for the tour saxophonist Sam Rivers, a rising free jazz star. Davis did so, but the two horn players failed to mesh musically or personally, with Rivers sharing Coleman's dislike of Miles' behavior. Back in the United States, Miles geared up to start a new phase in his career and went looking for a sax player who could help him achieve this.

Wayne Shorter, a thirty-one-year-old New Jersey native, had originally been recommended to Miles in 1960 by John Coltrane. Davis had hesitated then, but now, aware of how muscular Shorter's playing had grown during his time as a member of Art Blakey's Jazz Warriors, he made the call. Shorter accepted. Shorter's taut, melodic playing meshed brilliantly with the styles of Carter, Hancock, and Williams. Once again Miles displayed an extraordinary ability to find the best young musicians available. He now set about getting them to realize his new concepts, encouraging the young musicians to compose. In late January 1961, the Quintet entered the studio to record material for what would become the *E.S.P.* album.

The new quintet members came up with several strong tunes. Miles only contributed "Agitation" (and shared a co-writing credit on two Ron Carter compositions). *E.S.P.* is a radical departure from Davis' previous albums, the music's abstract, angular flavor, its nervous pulse and harsh tones, being both influenced by and a challenge to the free jazz scene then underway in New York. The album's cover featured a striking color photo of Miles studying his wife, Frances Davis. He looks handsome if tense, while she exudes the nervous tension of a deer caught in a hunter's rifle sights. "And that little face . . .," she later said, "You would not believe that about a week after it was taken I was running for my life."

Miles' father had died in 1962 and his mother passed in February 1964. Grief only intensified Miles' cocaine binges while his health worsened—the problems with his hip intensified to the point where he had trouble walking. A bone graft operation in April left him in a wheelchair for a time. In August, he broke his leg and while in the hospital had an operation for an artificial hip. By November, Miles was finally capable of undertaking regular work again. He became increasingly violent towards Frances, and when Davis returned home after a three-day cocaine binge and threatened her with a butcher's knife, she called the police and then slipped out once they arrived. Miles insisted—with threats, then pleas—that she return. But enough was enough, and the first Mrs. Miles Davis filed for divorce.

Miles performs at Shelley's Mann-Hole nightclub, Hollywood, California, in 1968. *Bettmann/Corbis*

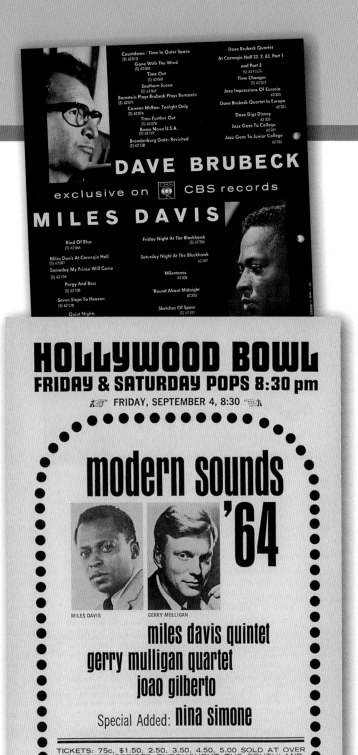

Advertisement, Hollywood Bowl, Hollywood,
California, September 4, 1964.

If Miles' personal life appeared in disarray, the Quintet were stretching their wings and learning to fly. In December 1965, Miles booked a residency at Chicago's Plugged Nickel club for the ensemble. He instructed Teo Macero to bring a recording truck to the venue, certain that the band should be captured in concert. Macero did so and then found Miles saying there would be no recording taking place as Williams—who, although still a teenager, appeared to be leading the Quintet—had insisted he did not want to record. Macero countered by stating that the cost of shipping all the recording equipment to Chicago would be charged against Miles' royalties. The trumpeter relented, and the recordings made on December 22 and 23, 1965, capture the Quintet in full flight, ranging through Miles' catalog and playing with such extraordinary grace that many aficionados consider the rhythm section of Williams–Carter–Hancock jazz's finest ever. The Plugged Nickel recordings lay dormant for many years—a single album appeared in Japan in 1976 and a double in the United States in 1982. Finally, in 1995, Sony released the entire Plugged Nickel live recordings as a remarkable eight-CD document.

In concert, Miles appeared reenergized by his young band, and with Williams setting the pace—the teenager's enthusiasm, vitality, and imagination made a change from the more jaded jazz musicians Miles was used to working with—the Quintet's sound became increasingly adventurous. Adventurous, but never as radical as the free jazz then burning up Manhattan nightclubs. Miles stretched his boundaries, yet never allowed the music to get so far out that he might lose his audience, especially seeing that his audience now included white nightclubs that paid very well. "Controlled freedom" is how he liked to describe his new sound. Herbie Hancock, then a free jazz disciple, called it "anti-music." Wayne Shorter was more circumspect, merely stating that they were "taking chances."

In 1964, the Beatles swept across the United States and rock 'n' roll went from being seen as music for juvenile delinquents to the hottest sound around. Miles, while always appreciating the blues, had previously sneered at rock 'n' roll. Yet Williams' enthusiasm for rock and the new funk sounds being developed by the likes of James Brown made Miles listen harder to what America's teenagers were dancing to.

In 1966, he turned forty and in February he was hospitalized for a liver infection. For three months he had to stay at home recuperating. Feeling his age and worrying about becoming irrelevant to younger audiences, he listened to the radio and heard rock start to take on psychedelic trimmings and new flavor by adding blues and soul, Indian sitar and jazz—the Los Angeles combo the Byrds borrowed the bass riff from John Coltrane's "A Love Supreme" for their hit "Eight Miles High." Detroit record label Motown unleashed hit after magnificent hit (the label's session musicians almost all being Detroit jazz players) while Memphis' Stax Records took deep Southern, gospel-flavored R&B high in the charts. "Soul music" people called it, and Miles, as ever, wanted to be the people's choice. But how?

As his liver healed, a young actress named Cicely Tyson came into Miles' life. Their on-off relationship would span three decades, and Tyson surely stands as the most defining female figure in Miles' life beyond his mother.

Back in the recording studio, the Quintet cut *Miles Smiles*. Again, they play with fierce joy, and the music mixes manic, fast blasts of sound with slower numbers that convey a coiled, mercurial intensity. Wayne Shorter compositions dominated *Miles Smiles*—Davis' sole composition, "Circle," featured him playing eloquent muted trumpet.

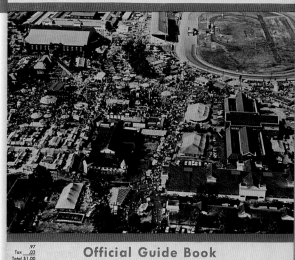

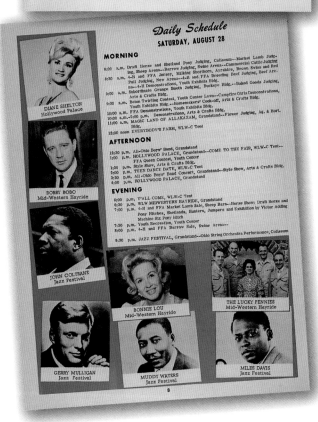

Program, Ohio State Fair, 1965.

In May 1967, the quintet recorded *Sorcerer*, an album, that when released in December, featured an intense, side-profile portrait of Cicely Tyson on the cover. *Sorcerer* is an uneven album, with Wayne Shorter contributing most of the tunes. By June 1967, Miles had the Quintet back in the studio to record an album that would be called *Nefertiti*. While a new Miles album now sold far less than *Kind of Blue* and *Sketches of Spain* did at the start of the decade, Columbia continued to believe in the trumpeter, aware they were working with a major artist. *Nefertiti* is considered by some to be the best album Miles cut with his youthful Quintet—Shorter contributed three strong tunes and the ensemble play superbly—but its March 1968 release attracted little attention.

The Quintet toured Europe in the autumn of 1967 to strong response. But while there, the bandmates also noticed how the new rock culture made jazz appear old-fashioned, a music for middle-aged intellectuals. Back in the United States, the Quintet began work on *Miles in the Sky* in January 1968, resuming sessions for two days in May with Miles inviting the hugely talented jazz guitarist George Benson to sit in. Benson contributed to "Paraphernalia" and found himself bemused—as many others had previously—by how Miles ran sessions: no instructions or suggests, just grunts, smiles, grimaces, and nods. Benson's contributions don't sit comfortably with what Shorter was attempting to achieve, yet Miles, searching for a new sound, invited him to join the band. Benson declined, going on to be a huge soul-jazz star in the 1970s.

Miles in the Sky is a tentative, unsatisfying album: Miles appears to be shedding his skin yet hasn't yet completed the process. By the time it was released in September, he had already reshuffled the band and moved on musically.

The recording sessions for the album that would be titled *Filles de Kilimanjaro*—Miles owned shares in a Tanzania coffee cooperative, thus the African reference (the French titles were a last minute idea of his)—began in June 1968 and resumed in September. By the time of the September sessions Ron Carter had quit—he disliked Miles' insistence that he play electric bass on all sessions—to be replaced by British bassist Dave Holland, while Herbie Hancock, on sick leave, was replaced by Chick Corea. Carter resumed his career as a leading session musician while Hancock, already an established solo artist, commented "It was like trying to make conversation never using any words you ever used before." Many listeners also felt that way, and Holland was amazed to find that even when playing long-established jazz clubs such as the Plugged Nickel, the audience often consisted of less than one hundred people.

Gil Evans helped considerably with *Filles de Kilimanjaro*, and the music has a languid, melodic texture thanks to him. It also has an earthy, bluesy texture: *Filles de Kilimanjaro* is where Miles begins to dive into jazz-rock fusion. The album's subtitle reads "Directions in Music by Miles Davis," and the trumpeter composed all five tunes.

The album's lengthiest track is "Mademoiselle Mabry," a tune about his latest beau, the twenty-three-year-old model and aspiring songwriter, Betty Mabry. Mabry also appeared on *Filles de Kilimanjaro*'s cover and by the time of the album's release in early 1969 she had become the second Mrs. Davis. But her influence on Miles' future directions were only just beginning.

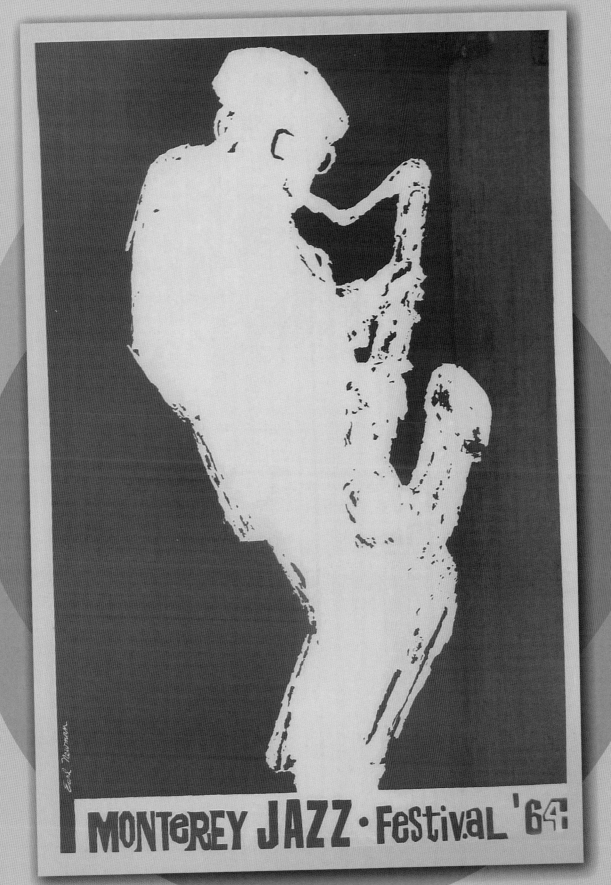

Poster, Monterey Jazz Festival, Monterey, California, 1964.

Miles plays in the spotlight at the Oriental Theater, Portland, Oregon, on May 21, 1966. His band at the time included Richard Davis on bass, replacing Ron Carter, and Herbie Hancock on piano. *David Hume Kennerly/Getty Images*

MILES AND THE 1960s QUINTET

by RON CARTER
and HERBIE HANCOCK

Bassist and cellist **RON CARTER** has played on more than 2,500 albums, including twelve albums with Miles Davis, beginning with *Quiet Nights* in 1962.

Keyboardist **HERBIE HANCOCK** joined Miles Davis' second great quintet in 1963 and played a starring role in redefining the jazz rhythm section and launching the post-bop sound.

Ron Carter: Every night with the Quintet felt like we were going to a laboratory. Miles was the head chemist and he would come out with these beakers full of liquid or powder, and it was our job to take these ingredients that he put on the table. *His* job was to keep up with us.

Sometimes we didn't do it right and sometimes he didn't do it right, but that was the fun of it all. No one cared if you didn't get the same reaction each night, or if you created an explosion, or somehow got the wrong results, we knew that tomorrow night was another chance to try to make something happen.

Herbie Hancock: It was incredible that this great musician had the balls to let us go that far just because we chose to, and we felt totally comfortable making that kind of commitment professionally on the stage with Miles as our leader. But the Quintet was not your typical leader plus sidemen situation. Miles' primary goal was to encourage all of us to contribute to the development of the sound of that band. Besides being the leader and the person with the overall vision, he was also one of the five musicians contributing to that evolution.

RC: We were all equal partners. Tony [Williams] was just as responsible as Wayne [Shorter], Herbie, Miles, and myself. He was one-fifth of this equation because the drums were a part of what the sound was. Besides missing him, it gets me kind of upset that he's not here to talk about those times, you know?

HH: The Quintet in 1964 was not the same band it became three or four years later. When Tony first joined, he sounded most comfortable when we were playing fast numbers; when we were playing moderate grooves, I felt his sound was not as effective. For almost two years, whatever tune we played, Miles would wind up doubling the tempo right after we played the melody. Everything was super-fast. It got to the point where Ron [Carter] and I started to rebel against that and we said to Miles that we didn't want to just race around.

But as Tony got older—I mean he was still young, six years younger than me, but he wasn't seventeen anymore—he started using heavier drumsticks and developed that style of playing the high hat on every beat. His musical development was coupled with his maturation as an adult, and he was able to find his own place in more moderate tempos and on ballads and still keep his sound.

There were no drummers out there doing any of the stuff that Tony was doing. The closest one I would say was Elvin Jones; he was playing with counter rhythms but musically most of what I heard from Elvin involved triplets. Tony was playing with much more complex things that involved phrases ending in five and seven and eleven, and looping those phrases, almost like in Indian music. He would start at the end of a chorus, he would play this thing in some other kind of meter and always wind up landing on its feet. Since then jazz musicians have done that kind of thing a lot but it really started with Tony.

I said, "I want to be able to do that with notes." That's one of the reasons I hung out with Tony a lot, besides the fact that I loved him like a brother. I was fascinated by what was coming out of him musically and I wanted to translate that into what I could do on the piano. I remember playing a concert in Europe somewhere, and I was soloing. At the end of one of the choruses I played some figure that had one of these magical, non-triplet, non-duple phrases that came out . . . bam . . . right on the one, where I was hoping it would come out. I was stunned I actually did that and I looked up at Tony and Tony just had a little smile on his face. He nodded his head, like a sign of approval—that I had gotten an A.

RC: When people ask if there was a secret to our creative process, my first answer is that we had a consistent library. When we first came together in 1964, we knew that the first song would usually be "Autumn Leaves" and the last song would generally be "Walkin'," and that "My Funny Valentine" and "If I Were A Bell" were almost always

"I knew right away that this was going to be a motherfucker of a group. For the first time in a while I found myself feeling excited inside, because if they were playing that good in a few days, what would they be playing like in a few months? . . . If I was the inspiration and wisdom and the link for this band, Tony [Williams] was the fire, the creative spark; Wayne [Shorter] was the idea person, the conceptualizer of a whole lot of musical ideas we did; and Ron [Carter] and Herbie [Hancock] were the anchors. I was just the leader who put us all together. Those were all young guys and although they were learning from me, I was learning from them, too, about the new thing, the free thing."

—**Miles Davis, *Miles: The Autobiography*, 1989**

Miles and his new Quartet take the stage, circa 1964. The Quartet included pianist Herbie Hancock, bassist Ron Carter, and drummer Tony Williams. *Michael Ochs Archives/Getty Images*

Poster, CBS Records, 1960s.

part of the set. Miles wanted us to learn this material and the more we played it, the more we got a chance to know it, and that gave us more options to experiment. What else can we do and still maintain the integrity of the melody, or of the form or of the changes?

HH: After Wayne joined the group, we grew to understand why, without having to ask Miles, certain standards were edited out of the repertoire. That was part of the development of the band; certain tunes, even if they had been favorites, didn't fit the direction of the band at the moment. They were structurally more restrictive than others, whether harmonically or rhythmically. Those that seemed to be more difficult to fit into our development went by the wayside.

RC: I think Miles kept some of those tunes around to let the audience know that as far out as we may get playing tunes like "Riot" or "Agitation," there was still the ability to play "I Fall In Love Too Easily" or "Stella By Starlight." We could play those tunes with the same amount of freedom as the newer songs, plus we understood that because this is a song that everyone knows, let's see what we can do

and still have them hear "My Funny Valentine." I think Miles was very aware of it effect on an audience.

HH: Miles had a very acute sense of programming—what tunes would work in front of an audience as part of an hour-and-a-half performance or whatever. You have to figure out what's going to work as an opening song, as a set-closer, and you follow that instinct.

RC: For us—well, definitely for me— those familiar standards were also chance to be less concerned about finding something slick to do, and just find a great half note and not worry about beats three and four. I think it also allowed Herbie to breathe a little more comfortably without us marching up his back, and it allowed Tony to play brushes and not worry about getting lost in the form. I think we all needed that at certain moments. But at the same time, I did not have a problem with the enthusiasm that "Footprints" would bring.

Miles blows his trumpet with Wayne Shorter on saxophone and Herbie Hancock on piano in Berlin, Germany, 1964. *JazzSign/Lebrecht Music & Arts/Corbis*

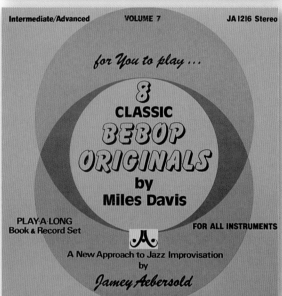

HH: I particularly liked Wayne's compositions, like "Dolores" or "Masqualero." They really captured the new sound of the Quintet, and had the kind of openness and originality that defined the spirit of that band. "Footprints" was especially interesting because it had just enough structure to relate it to what Miles had done before but there was inherently enough freedom in it to bridge both eras.

I know Miles liked Wayne's tunes because though they were written they still gave him a lot of freedom to respond to the moment. And that moment could be influenced by how he was feeling that night or the sound of the band at that time. Or by other events, you know? I mean culturally that happens anyway in works of art but especially in jazz.

RC: See, I think people misunderstand what jazz improvisation is. I believe the great players are the ones who stumble onto an idea on Tuesday and on Wednesday they develop it. They're not necessarily looking for new notes or a new set of changes every night. It isn't so much a matter of reinventing as having the memory to build on something that they or someone else played the previous night.

So much of this depended on staying focused on what we were doing from song to song. I think that's one reason Miles started moving straight from one tune to the next, not waiting for one to end before starting another. I think what those segues tended to do is nail them to their seats—often, the audience didn't quite know if it was time to applaud. Good, don't applaud because something else is coming up. Applause can be like call waiting, you know, interrupting our flow of thought.

HH: I never really focused that much on why Miles would start into the next tune before we'd actually get to an ending of the first one and I don't remember exactly when Miles started that, other than it was after Wayne came into the band. But I think it went along with the evolution of the sound of the band—our sound came from the individual input of the five musicians. That was another of Miles' contributions. It was all part of the soup, just another spice that made it all work so well together.

Starting in the late 1950s, various recordings of Miles' solos were transcribed and offered to trumpet players eager to imitate or examine his playing.

Miles, circa 1965. *Gai Terrell/Redferns*

MILES AND THE BALLADS

by FRANCIS DAVIS

FRANCIS DAVIS is the jazz critic for the *Village Voice* and a contributing editor for the *Atlantic Monthly*. He is the author of numerous books on jazz and the blues, including *Bebop and Nothingness: Jazz and Pop at the End of the Century*.

So much of what we think we know about Miles Davis as a player (much less what we assume we know about him as a man) turns out to be . . . not wrong, exactly, but richer and more complicated than legend allows. It's often said, for example, that Miles, who was barely out of his teens when he began recording with Charlie Parker in 1946, and unable to match Dizzy Gillespie and Fats Navarro for speed and altitude, didn't become his own man on trumpet until forming his own soft-hued nonet three years later. And there's some truth to this—Miles frequently sounds thrown for a loop trying to keep pace with Parker on fast tempos. But his confident and wounded choruses on the ballads he recorded with Parker tell an altogether different story.

I once heard Woody Shaw say that he and Freddie Hubbard were branches on the mighty oak that spouted from Louis Armstrong and had earlier given growth to Roy Eldridge and Dizzy. Sure, I remember thinking, and by that logic, Miles was Isaac Newton sitting in the shade waiting for the apple to drop. Miles had his own conception right from the start, but until he was able to create his own context, it was a conception that required the gravitational pull of a slow tempo to articulate itself clearly. "Don't Blame Me" and "My Old Flame," both with Parker from 1947, were merely the earliest in what proved to be a career-long succession of ballad performances as masterful and compelling as any by Billie Holiday, Frank Sinatra, or Jeri Southern (Miles' surprising choice as Best Female Singer in a 1956 musicians' poll conducted by Leonard Feather).

Along with Johnny Hodges, Ben Webster, Stan Getz, Lester Young, and Bobby Hackett (another Miles favorite), Miles was among a handful of great jazz instrumentalists who were singers by other means. "I didn't learn to phrase by listening to other trumpet players," he told the British music critic Roy Carr in 1986. "From the very start, I learnt phrasing from listening to all of Sinatra's early recordings. No singer has ever bettered those albums he made for Capitol with Nelson Riddle and Gordon Jenkins." Unless it was Southern—whose close miking Miles may have consciously emulated in the studio and whose LPs he reportedly devoured (along with Sinatra's) for songs he himself might record—nobody "sang" "Something I Dreamed

Last Night" more wistfully than Miles did on his version for Prestige in 1956.

That song happens to be a favorite of mine, but around the same time, Miles recorded a number of others that could serve just as well as examples. On his 1950s Prestige dates, ballads were Miles' star turn. Not even Coltrane, who was no slouch as a crooner himself, was invited to share the spotlight—at least not until Miles began to exploit the tension implicit in their different approaches to slow tempos after switching labels. Miles became Columbia's hipper, modernist alternative to Hackett and Jonah Jones, swing trumpeters whose albums of "muted" jazz were hot items in 1950s bachelor pads. But unlike Hackett's or Jones', Miles' muted ballad solos never consisted mostly of embellishment or melodic paraphrase. Like Parker's (or, for that matter, Sarah Vaughan's), they amounted to full-blown thematic variations. Although never merely pretty, and too spiked with apparent fluffs to be relaxing, they played a sizeable part in gaining Miles celebrity outside the circumscribed world of jazz. (Knowledgeable sources say he was the model for the character Shago Martin, the epitome of black cool with whom a Norman Mailer surrogate overcomes "some hard-lodged fear I have always felt with Negroes" by beating him to a pulp and throwing him down a flight of stairs in Mailer's 1965 novel *An American Dream*. In real life, the two had been rivals for Carol Stevens, later Mailer's fifth wife.)

With the hornet's buzz of his mute serving a distancing purpose similar to Southern's lisp—keeping us at arm's length even while daring to expose a vulnerability—Miles' ballads went a long way in establishing his mystique. Drawing us closer but always holding something back (and not just the beat), they gave us Miles close-up, but as if in three-quarter profile. His way with ballads also helps explain why he enjoyed a larger female following than any jazz instrumentalist before or since. To say that ballads put Miles in touch with his feminine side would be opening a can of Freudian worms better left in the pantry, given his rumored bisexuality and scientific debate over whether characterological traits are truly gender-specific. Still, could anyone else have convincingly "sung" both leads in *Porgy and Bess*, as Miles did with Gil Evans?

Dressing sharp as usual, Miles performs at the Newport Jazz Festival on July 4, 1966. Bassist Ron Carter and drummer Tony Williams back him. *Gai Terrell/Redferns*

The question naturally occurs why someone so gifted at interpreting ballads would suddenly just give them up. Though "I Fall In Love Too Easily" remained in Miles' set list as late as 1970, the 1964 live album *My Funny Valentine* was effectively his Goodbye to All That. Perhaps it was nothing more than finding two of the era's most ambitious and prolific composers in his employ, in Shorter and Hancock. But a better answer might be found by considering the question within the larger framework of an identity crisis in 1960s and early-1970s adult pop. Sinatra was recording "Something" and "Bad, Bad Leroy Brown," Streisand and Ella were covering Laura Nyro and Randy Newman, respectively, and Mel Tormé was doing what he could with "If I Had A Hammer" and "Secret Agent Man." Numbers like "Stella By Starlight" and "On Green Dolphin Street" weren't on anyone's lips (except as a sneer) at the Fillmores when Miles crashed that circuit with *Bitches Brew*, nor would such numbers have earned him much cred on black street corners, where he ultimately wanted his music to land. In *Miles: The Autobiography*, Miles throws us off the trail by alleging he couldn't play love songs unless he was in love. More likely, he loved certain *songs* too much to waste them on younger audiences dismissive of them—or, as Keith Jarrett once suggested, to hear them mishandled by younger musicians unfamiliar with them.

But hold on. Who says Miles ever stopped playing ballads? This is another of those prevalent half-truths. Standards, sure, but not what dancers on *Bandstand* used to call "slow songs" or what I've heard musicians refer to as "downtempo." Any number of Miles' own compositions from 1966 on, beginning with "Circle," from *Miles Smiles*, qualify as "ballads" by this expanded definition, and so do the pop hits he made his own in the 1980s—even if bubble gum like Cyndi Lauper's "Time After Time," Michael Jackson's "Human Nature," and Scritti Politti's "Perfect Way" gave him almost nothing to chew on harmonically (and even if the studio versions have none of the emotional drive they acquired once he'd roadtested them in concert).

I heard Miles live at least once annually in the years following his last comeback in 1982, and I swear he played the same exact set the last three times. In 1989, I think it was, his opening act was Kenny G., who silenced demand for a second encore by telling his fans, "I don't know about you, but I can't wait to hear Miles Davis." I gave Mr. G. points for graciousness, but it was a sad reminder that time was marching on. To what proved the final Miles concert I would attend, I took as my plus-one a woman with an eye for color and fabric and gave her the job to describe to me what Miles was wearing, so I'd have something new to report in the next morning's paper. All I remember now is that his shirt and trousers were loose and flowing, and all that billow made him look shrunken and brittle.

But there turned out to be no need to mention his stage wardrobe in my review, because Miles was still Miles when it counted—when he'd pick up on a guitar riff and start slow jamming a blues, or even better, as he paced the stage worrying over the melody of "Time After Time," promising us and maybe even delivering a glimpse beneath the cool. It didn't matter whether the song was one you liked, nor how many times before you'd heard him play it. Miles' ballads cut deep, right to the end.

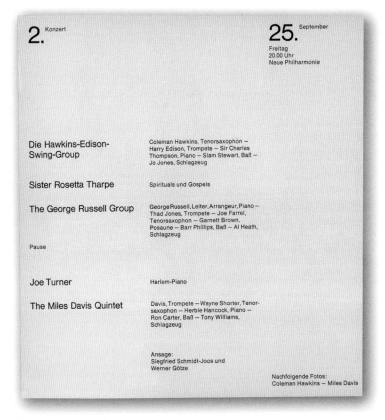

Program and poster, Berliner Jazz Tage, 1964.

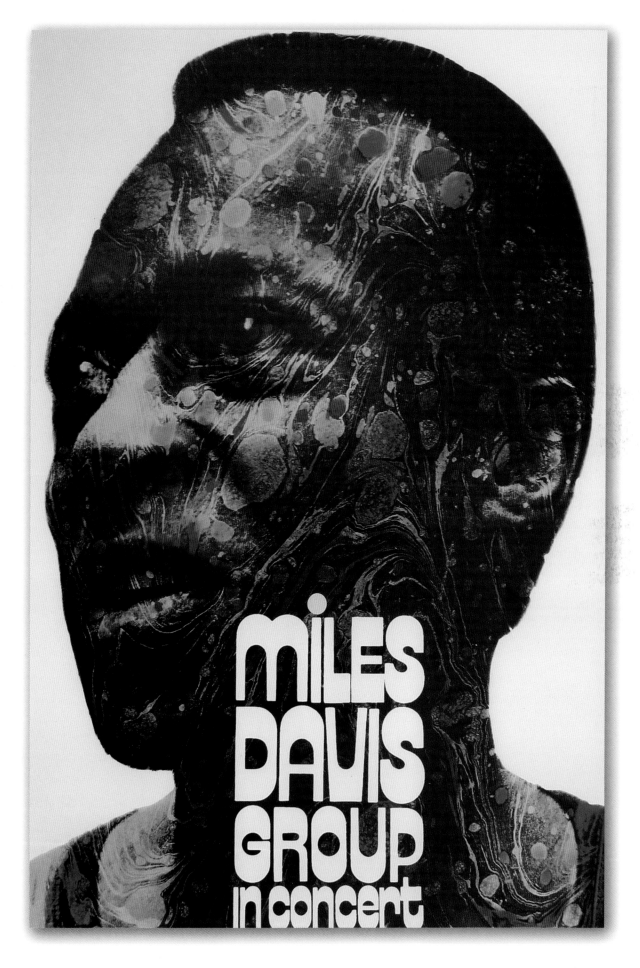

6

Bitches Brew And Beyond

1969–1974

With his amplified trumpet and wah-wah pedal, Miles performs in Copenhagen, Denmark, on October 29, 1973.
Jan Persson/Redferns/Getty Images

AS 1969 DAWNED, MILES DAVIS' YOUNG WIFE BETTY was determined to hip him to the counterculture and what was going on in soul and rock. Not that she had to try hard—Miles was sick of jazz with its neat suits, empty clubs, dismal record sales, and aging audience. He wanted to go where the action was. And Betty, a tough talking beauty with a huge afro and chic wardrobe, knew where to look. Already a face on the New York scene, Betty hung out in the hippest clubs, befriending musicians alongside the counterculture's movers and shakers. She quickly changed her husband's dress sense—the classic Brooks Brothers suits were replaced by kaftans, sunglasses, baggy pants, and silk shifts. And she pointed him toward the most happening musicians.

Miles, normally so willful, paid attention. Even in the jazz world his status had slipped—John Coltrane had caused a much greater impact with his 1964 album *A Love Supreme* than anything released by Davis across the decade. Coltrane, who died unexpectedly in 1967 of liver disease, now existed as free jazz's potent icon, his radical approach to making music—and the spiritual yearning at the heart of his quest—connecting with a younger audience. Heading in the opposite direction, Cannonball Adderley's funky soul-jazz hit the R&B charts and won a young black fanbase. This was a fanbase that Miles constantly felt frustrated at his failure to reach. Indeed, when Leonard Feather—the great doyen of American jazz writers—visited Miles he was shocked to find records by the Byrds, Aretha Franklin, Fifth Dimension, James Brown, and Dionne Warwick. But no jazz LPs.

Most distinctive of these artists to Miles' future development was Georgia R&B veteran James Brown. Brown had stripped rhythm and blues down to its core elements, thus creating funk, an American music truly African in groove. And his ferocious band featured several jazz musicians who blended percussion and horns to great effect. Miles also confessed to being impressed by Sly Stone and Jimi Hendrix—Sly had taken Brown's funky soul sound and dusted it with hippie vibes while Hendrix, a veteran of the chitlin' circuit's R&B bands, embraced psychedelic rock and rewrote the possibilities of electric guitar. Young audiences loved these pioneers of a new African American music, and Miles wanted the same. Jazz, he decided, was dead. In a 1969 interview with Les Tomkins, Miles stated, "Jazz is an Uncle Tom word. They should stop using that word for selling. I told George Wein the other day that he should stop using it."

For nearly twenty years, Miles had been the alpha male of American jazz and, now middle-aged, he hated feeling left behind. He disliked feeling old and in the way. Jazz saxophonist Charles Lloyd had successfully crossed over to the psychedelic rock audience, and Miles also wanted to be a player. His rage to make music that mattered, to lead rather than follow, found forceful expression on February 2, 1969, when he entered a New York studio accompanied by Tony Williams, Dave Holland, Wayne Shorter, and Chick Corea. He also invited along Herbie Hancock—the two musicians remained cordial—and Josef Zawinul, the Austrian keyboardist who, as part of Cannonball's band, had provided Adderley with his biggest hit, "Mercy Mercy Mercy." Miles had very definite ideas of what he wanted, designating acoustic and electric piano and organ duties to the trio.

The night before they entered the studio, Miles had gone to Count Basie's club in Harlem to watch Tony Williams jam with John McLaughlin, a twenty-seven-year-old British guitarist who had just flown into New York to form Lifetime with the drummer. Miles was impressed by McLaughlin and, much to Williams' chagrin, invited the guitarist to join them in the studio.

McLaughin had many years' experience under his belt, having played on plenty of sessions and, as a teenager, shared the stage with Ginger Baker and Jack Bruce long before Eric Clapton joined them to form Cream. His debut solo album *Extrapolation* had only been released a month or so before he left for New York and it had already been hailed as "the best British jazz album ever." Miles had already auditioned and dismissed several guitarists, and McLaughlin, aware the trumpeter was looking for that "something else" (while being unsure of exactly what this was), felt understandably nervous.

The good life: Miles rests on his Lamborghini Miura S, circa 1970. *Mark Patiky/ Condé Nast Archive/Corbis*

Poster, Monterey Jazz Festival, Monterey, California, September 19–21, 1969.

Poster, New York Pop, Downing Stadium,
Randall's Island, New York, July 17–19, 1970.

Zawinul, who grew up in Vienna, Austria, of mixed Czech, Hungarian, and Romany bloodlines, began playing accordion as a child, learning Turkish, Romanian, and Gypsy folk music. Although born into a poor family, his musical prowess meant he got a scholarship to study classical music at an academy. As a teenager Zawinul saw the film *Stormy Weather* twenty-four times and determined that one day he too would play jazz with African Americans. Zawinul arrived in the United States on a scholarship to study at Berklee College of Music in Boston, in 1959. He lasted a week, then lit out on the road, backing the likes of Dinah Washington. Miles had long admired Zawinul's skills as a musician and composer, and he invited him to the recording only a short time before, telling him to bring a keyboard and some compositions. "In A Silent Way" was one of these compositions, Zawinul having written it with Miles in mind.

In the studio, Miles gave his usual minimal instructions. He eliminated chords from "In A Silent Way," and told McLaughlin to play the melody on a single chord, adding "play the guitar like you don't know how to play." Recording started immediately— no rehearsals—and McLaughlin noted that when producer Teo Macero played the recording back he found himself shocked at how Miles had "made me play in a way that I had not been aware of."

The session moved quickly with Shorter playing soprano saxophone for the first time, Zawinul on organ while Corea and Hancock played keyboards. Williams played a hi-hat pattern that shuffles brilliantly throughout the recording. Corea later stated how the assembled musicians all thought they had just had a run-through of Zawinul's tune "but it turned out to be the finished product."

With Miles directing, everyone then worked on a number of short pieces that Macero would later carefully edit and assemble into the eighteen-minute track "Shhh/Peaceful" and "It's About That Time," an eleven-minute piece sandwiched in between "In A Silent Way" and a reprise of "In A Silent Way," Macero looping Zawinul's four-minute tune to close out the album. Richard Cook would note, "The two pieces they recorded that day more or less announced the revolution."

"What we did on *Bitches Brew* you couldn't ever write down for an orchestra to play. That's why I didn't write it all out, not because I didn't know what I wanted; I knew that what I wanted would come out of a process and not some prearranged shit. This session was about improvisation, and that's what makes jazz so fabulous."

—Miles Davis, *Miles: The Autobiography*, 1989

If they did signal a revolution, the American public were circumspect. Jazz critics tended to dismiss *In a Silent Way*, yet the album quickly shifted ninety thousand copies—nothing comparable to what the big rock and soul stars were selling but more than double the sales of any of Miles' albums over the past five years. A younger audience, hearing *In a Silent Way* on the new freeform FM radio stations, liked it—possibly as a soundtrack to getting stoned—and *Rolling Stone*, then a fledgling underground newspaper, assigned the review to Lester Bangs, a twenty-year-old with a huge passion for rock and jazz. Bangs wrote of *In a Silent Way*, "It is neither jazz nor rock . . . I believe there is a new music in the air, a total art which knows no boundaries or categories, a new school indifferent to fashion." Bangs' enthusiasm wasn't just hyperbole. *In a Silent Way*'s gentle intensity would quietly influence experimental music making—jazz and rock, ambient and classical.

In a Silent Way allowed Miles to claw back some degree of status and he wasted no time. On August 13, 1969, he took thirteen musicians—including Corea, Zawinul, Hancock, Shorter, Holland, and McLaughlin—into a New York studio for three days of controlled chaos. For the *Bitches Brew* recordings, Miles broke his long-standing rule of no partners at the sessions and brought Betty along, glancing at her for approval. He divided the musicians between percussion and brass–guitar–keyboards, then directed them in his typically oblique manner. They played loud, grasping at whatever possibilities Miles offered them, creating long jams. Teo Macero recorded everything and then set about editing the jams, splicing the dissonant snorts and blasts into a double album that begins with "Pharoah's Dance," a twenty-minute-long riff on a Joe Zawinul tune, then followed with Davis' twenty-seven-minute title track. Three more Davis "compositions" followed with one—"John McLaughlin," a four-minute slice of guitar wizardry, being an edit from the jam that became the title track—before Wayne Shorter's "Sanctuary" closed proceedings. Shorter's composition was the closest thing to jazz on the album, finding Miles and keyboardist Chick Corea dueting.

Recording for BBC television's "Jazz Scene" at Ronnie Scott's Jazz Club in London on November 2, 1969, Miles leads his band, including Chick Corea on a Fender Rhodes electric piano, bassist Dave Holland, and drummer Jacques de Johnette. *David Redfern/Redferns*

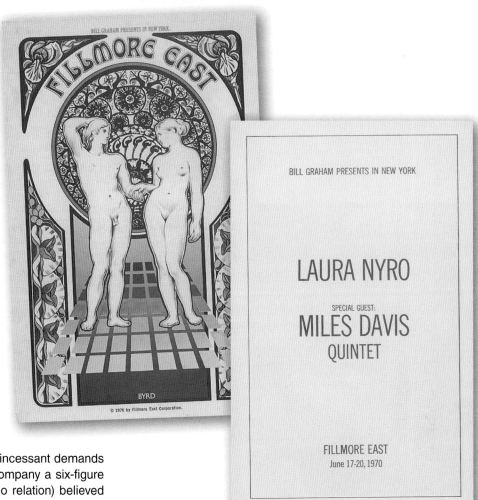

BILL GRAHAM PRESENTS IN NEW YORK

LAURA NYRO

SPECIAL GUEST:
MILES DAVIS
QUINTET

FILLMORE EAST
June 17-20, 1970

Program, Fillmore East, June 17–20, 1970.

Columbia had begun to tire of Miles' incessant demands for money—he already owed the company a six-figure sum. But label head Clive Davis (no relation) believed in Miles and angled him towards rock audiences. Clive Davis' suggestion that Miles play Bill Graham's celebrated venue the Fillmore East in New York initially offended Miles so deeply he demanded that the label release him but, as was often the case, he reconsidered, and signed up to open for the Steve Miller Band and Neil Young on March 6 and 7, 1970. The audience responded favorably to the electronic storm on stage—thirty-one years later the concert recordings would be released as *It's About That Time*—and the chance to play at rock concert volume and employ such Hendrix-approved "guitar effects" as a wah-wah pedal and Echoplex on his trumpet's signal appealed to Miles. Not that he thought much about his fellow musicians on the bill, telling an interviewer, "I remember one time—it might have been a couple times—at the Fillmore East in 1970, I was opening for this sorry-ass cat named Steve Miller. Steve Miller didn't have his shit going for him, so I'm pissed because I got to open for this non-playing motherfucker just because he had one or two sorry-ass records out. So I would come late and he would have to go on first and then we got there we smoked the motherfucking place, everybody dug it."

Released in January 1970, *Bitches Brew*, from its music to its psychedelic sleeve design by the Israeli artist Mati Klarwein, was a scorched-earth war on jazz tradition. Miles and Macero had created ninety minutes of contemporary urban music that alienated jazz's old guard while reaching a young audience—*Bitches Brew* quickly sold more than four hundred thousand copies. The transformation was complete.

Miles having successfully shed his jazz skin, he also shed Betty. The headstrong couple divorced after only one year; basically, Betty was too wild for Miles. She would go on to release four albums of savage funk across the early 1970s and, belatedly, be championed as a pioneer of sorts by funk-rock bands and female rappers. Miles found new lovers in Jackie Battle and Marguerite Eskridge, a Native American woman who would give birth to Miles' fourth and final child, a boy named Erin. Not that Miles' life had become any calmer—in October 1969, five bullets were shot at Miles and Marguerite, one grazing Davis, in what appears to have been a warning by Mafia-linked club owners, or drug dealers, or black nationalists unhappy at the trumpeter's willingness to play venues owned by whites (Miles believed the latter). Davis' ability to upset rarely left him: To celebrate Louis Armstrong's seventieth birthday, *Down Beat* magazine asked scores of leading jazz musicians to pay tribute, and Miles struck the only sour note, observing of the man whose music had so influenced him, "his personality was developed by white people wanting black people to entertain by smiling and jumping around."

Zawinul and Shorter, both unenthusiastic about how Miles had approached recording their compositions, left his employ and formed Weather Report, the jazz fusion band who enjoyed

Poster, Allen Theatre, Cleveland, Ohio, November 1, 1970.

immense success across the 1970s. Davis barely noticed, bringing in Indian and Brazilian musicians to add ethnic flavors to his sonic stew. The harsh guitar tones featured on *Bitches Brew* suggested Miles remained in thrall to Jimi Hendrix, and he spoke several times of his dream of recording with the guitarist. How much this was simply Miles extrapolating for the media no one can say—Hendrix producer Alan Douglas labored for months to set up a recording session between the two and on the day it was set to happen Miles rang and demanded $50,000 before he would set foot in the studio. Another time Hendrix followed up an invitation to jam with Miles, only to arrive at his apartment and find Davis absent, having left sheet music on a stand for Jimi to learn (Hendrix did not read music and Miles, ever wanting to unsettle, knew this). Miles and Sly Stone did hang out together—both men shared similar personalities and cocaine addictions—but there was too much ego in the room for the two to ever work together.

In April 1970, a studio jam between John McLaughlin, Herbie Hancock, drummer Billy Cobham, soprano sax player Steve Grossman, and twenty-year-old electric bassist Michael Henderson (already a veteran of Stevie Wonder's band and soon to become Miles' mainstay for the rest of the 1970s) became the basis for Miles' 1971 album *A Tribute to Jack Johnson*. The album was commissioned as a soundtrack to a documentary film about the legendary heavyweight boxing champion, and Miles, a boxing aficionado, enthusiastically embraced the project, studying old fight footage, drawing parallels between himself and Johnson—both loved fast cars, fast women, and refused to show respect to white authorities. As the jam took shape Miles ran out of the studio's control room and began blowing superb trumpet, his sharp, deft notes on "Right Off," jabbing at McLaughlin's guitar. The twenty-five minute epic "Yesternow" is less turbulent, more reflective—Macero edited into this tune a brief trumpet solo from 1969's "Shhh/Peaceful" and a recording made in February when Miles jammed with guitarist Sonny Sharrock; McLaughlin and other members of his band who were not present at the April recording. *Jack Johnson* is a tougher, more focused jazz-rock album than *Bitches Brew*, the musicians and Macero avoiding that album's occasionally turgid pace. Commercially, *Jack Johnson* came nowhere near matching *Bitches Brew* but it stands as Miles' most visceral album. And one of his finest.

Tickets, Fillmore West, San Francisco, California, April 9–12, 1970.

On August 29, 1970, Miles played the Isle of Wight Festival in England. Here, in front of the largest audience—six hundred thousand strong—he would ever face, Davis appeared alongside the likes of Jimi Hendrix, the Doors, the Who, and Sly & the Family Stone, so establishing his new music as part of the counterculture's soundtrack.

The double album *Live-Evil*, recorded in New York and Washington, D.C., nightclubs in 1970 (released in late 1971), found Miles incorporating compositions by Brazil's Hermeto Pascoal alongside several long, dense jazz-rock jams. Keith Jarrett, a prodigiously gifted pianist who would soon go on to remarkable solo fame, joined the group on keyboards and organ. Jarrett's fluid, experimental playing initially complemented that of Corea's, but once Corea left, Jarrett reverted to a more traditional role, and soon made it clear that while he admired Miles, he disliked the band and the loud fusion they were playing.

With the 1972 album *On the Corner*, Miles announced he would play "that roadhouse, honky-tonk, funky thing that people used to dance to on Friday night" to connect him to a young black audience. Miles then went about doing this in a manner that held almost no appeal to funk fans. Choosing to incorporate the method and music of German avant-garde composer Karlheinz Stockhausen, *On the Corner* features rumbling bass riffs and dense percussion while horns and guitars, sitars and keyboards are smeared across this sonic collage. Critically scorned and a commercial failure, *On the Corner* now enjoys cult status with avant-rockers and experimental DJs embracing its hypnotic rhythms and churning soundscape. But for most of Miles' audience, new and old, *On the Corner*'s absence of recognizable jazz trumpet and its dissonant atmosphere were a step too far.

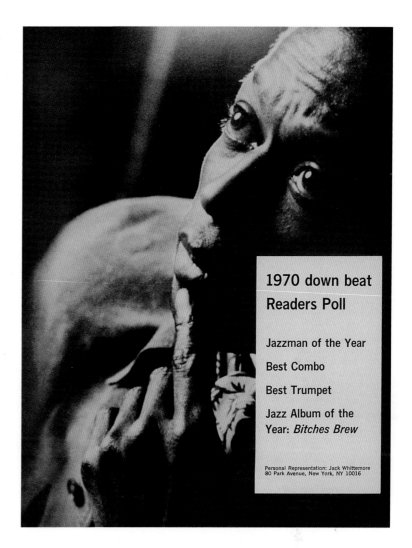

1970 down beat
Readers Poll

Jazzman of the Year

Best Combo

Best Trumpet

Jazz Album of the
Year: *Bitches Brew*

Personal Representation: Jack Whittemore
80 Park Avenue, New York, NY 10016

"That's the way electronics came to me. First I got a Fender bass, then a piano, and then I had to play my trumpet against that. So then I got an amplifier hook-up with a microphone on my trumpet. Then I got the wah-wah to make me sound more like a guitar. . . . Playing the new shit was gradual process. You just don't stop playing the way you used to play. You don't hear the sound at first. It takes time. When you do hear the new sound, it's like a rush, but a slow rush."

—**Miles Davis**, *Miles: The Autobiography*, **1989**

Handbill, Schaefer Music Festival, Harvard Stadium, Boston, Massachusetts, July 8, 1970.

"I was getting away from using a lot of solos in my group sound, moving more toward an ensemble thing, like the funk and rock bands."

—Miles Davis, *Miles: The Autobiography*, 1989

This rejection, aligned with a sugar-heavy diet and substance abuse, found Miles physically ailing. He kept touring, but was often hospitalized, his chaotic lifestyle causing him to crash his car and break both ankles, be arrested for drug possession, and descend further into paranoia. "Everything started to blur after that car accident," Miles later reflected, and so it seemed. Many musicians passed through his band, and guitarist Pete Cosey, a veteran of Chicago blues label Chess, added fierce dynamics. Watching his former sidemen enjoy huge success with their fusion outfits (Weather Report, Return to Forever, the Headhunters, Mahavishnu Orchestra) only fed Miles' rage, especially when he had to open concerts for them. On stage, he often turned his back on the audience—whether out of contempt or to direct his musicians has been debated—while his powerful band (up to nine musicians), most of them now from rock and funk backgrounds, played loud. Miles channeled his amplified trumpet through a wah-wah pedal, making his sound ever more intense. Yet he failed to replicate *Bitches Brew*'s success. Jack Bruce noted, "Miles wants to be Jimi Hendrix, but he can't work it out on trumpet."

The year 1974 saw Columbia release two Miles Davis double albums: the uneven *Big Fun* gathered unreleased recordings from 1969, 1970, and 1972, while the superior *Get Up With It* mixed recordings from 1970, 1972, and 1973 with three new recordings. These new tunes were his quietest since "In A Silent Way" and included Davis' thirty-two-minute-long homage to the late Duke Ellington, "He Loved Him Madly." If Ellington's passing made Miles reflect on loss, the taciturn trumpeter might have noted that Paul Chambers had died (of tuberculosis) in 1969 and Wynton Kelly (of epilepsy) in 1971, while Jimi Hendrix had choked to death on his own vomit. If Miles was trying to communicate on grief and pain, few appeared to be listening.

Isolated, ill, and paranoid, Miles began to withdraw from the world.

Miles performs with saxophonist Gary Bartz at the Tanglewood Music Festival in Lenox, Massachusetts, in August 1970. *David Gahr/Getty Images*

Miles plays the Isle of Wight Festival, on August 29, 1970. *David Redfern/Redferns*

MILES, TONY WILLIAMS, *AND* THE *ROAD* TO BITCHES BREW

by LENNY WHITE

Drummer **LENNY WHITE** played on Miles Davis' *Bitches Brew*. He went on to join Chick Corea's Return to Forever.

To understand *Bitches Brew* you have to understand that the first notes we made in the studio happened twenty-four hours after the last note Jimi Hendrix played at Woodstock. There were a lot of different kinds of music being made at the same time. You had Jimi Hendrix, you still had the Beatles, Igor Stravinsky, James Brown. You had Santana, the Rolling Stones—all this different music at the same time. You could hear that jazz was cross-pollinating—things being borrowed from here, from there. Everybody was listening to everybody else.

Jazz drumming in the 1960s was on fire—moving from a swinging pulse to a much more open, syncopated feel. We were listening to James Brown and his drummers—Clyde Stubblefield, Jabo Starks, Bernard Purdie. Sly & the Family Stone—their music was very influential too.

Jazz drummers were influenced by all this, but we didn't do it the same way. With jazz, the syncopation is not that repetitive. That groove is constantly growing and building on whatever you did in the last two bars and then something else happens, and that's what makes it so interesting. With *Bitches Brew* for example, each track became interesting organically.

With us young drummers around New York, there were two schools of jazz drumming at this time: the Miles school and the Trane school, so between Tony Williams and Elvin Jones, that was it. In the neighborhood, either you were with one or the other. I was seventeen years old in 1967 when I heard Miles' "Seven Steps to Heaven" and found out that Tony was seventeen when he made that record! Right away he became my guy.

To me Tony was the catalyst of Miles' band—he was the guy who turned Miles' head around. He's not given enough credit for that. I think that Miles was getting off hearing what Tony was hearing in the music, and was opening up their music for him to play. Tony was with Miles from the age of seventeen to twenty-three. In those few years, the records that he made changed drumming. Not just drumming, they changed musical styles.

You can trace the development of Tony's approach through different tracks on Miles' albums—from "Gingerbread Boy" on *Miles Smiles*, then "Nerfertiti" from *Nefertiti*, which was basically a feature for the rhythm section, the horns just play the melody over and over again. Tony played some unbelievable stuff, but always within the framework of the music. He didn't play something just to play it. Then "Stuff" on *Miles in the Sky*, and then "Frelon Brun" or "Tout de Suite" on *Filles de Kilimanjaro*.

No band is better than its drummer and Miles knew that. In Miles' bands no drummer had his hands tighter on the steering wheel in respect to the direction of the music than Tony. Remember at the same time there was the avant-garde movement in jazz. There was a cross between the traditional and the avant-garde, and it was all moving someplace else.

There's another key to understanding *Bitches Brew*: in 1969, Tony had the idea to take a traditional concept—the standard organ trio—and put it on steroids. He formed Tony Williams Lifetime with John McLaughlin and Larry Young, and it became the new way, the new movement. I saw that group at Slug's when they first started—it was so great and SO LOUD. They were so good Miles wanted to hire Tony's band and call it, "Miles Davis introduces Tony Williams Lifetime." Tony said no, he didn't want to do that. So Miles went ahead and got Larry and John for *Bitches Brew*. Tony was not happy with that but I think he had definitely made the decision to go off on his own by then anyway.

When I got to the studio for *Bitches Brew*, I remember Jack had on sunglasses. Miles came to me and said, "Look, Jack's wearing the shades so he's going to be the leader. He's going to play the beat, I want you to play all around the beat." I still laugh about that.

That was my role: to play in between the cracks. I wanted it to sound like one drummer with eight hands. You know, some critics say Jack played by himself on "Sanctuary" but it's not true, yet I consider that a compliment in a way. I played subtly and it sounds like it's just one guy.

Bassist Dave Holland, Miles, and Chick Corea perform at the Longhorn Jazz Festival in Dallas Texas, on July 18, 1969. *Tad Hershorn/Hulton Archive/Getty Images*

Advertisement, Royce Hall, University of California–Los Angeles, October 10, 1970.

See, in the true African tradition, there could be thirty drummers or more in one village. And there's an adage that says if you're in a group like that and you can hear yourself, you're not swinging.

The entire group was built around a double rhythm section—two drummers; two percussionists; two bassists; two, sometimes three, keyboards; *and* guitar! We were all positioned in a semi-circle with Miles and Wayne in the middle. Miles would start a take by pointing at someone, like John or Jack, we'd all play and then he'd stop us with a wave of his hand.

Every take was different, that's what I mean by organic—you'd do it one way and then the next time it was off in a totally different direction. And they weren't what you would call complete takes, like on *Kind of Blue*, with a beginning, middle, and end. The closest to that was "Sanctuary" or "Spanish Key"; even then an entire section might be edited out, like with "Pharaoh's Dance."

My kit was right next to Jack, which was perfect since I really had to adapt my playing and my mindset to fit into this giant rhythmic sound. There was a huge chance it could break down into cacophony, but there was such a high level of intelligence in that room. It's definitely a testament to Miles' ability to choose people who could communicate with minimal direction, without words. We were all speaking the same language. You can hear it in the music.

ISLE OF WIGHT FESTIVAL
AUGUST 26-30 1970

FRIDAY 28th
CHICAGO
FAMILY
TASTE
PROCOL HARUM
JAMES TAYLOR
ARRIVAL
MELANIE
VOICES OF
EAST HARLEM
LIGHTHOUSE

WEEKEND £3

SATURDAY 29th
THE DOORS
THE WHO
TEN YEARS AFTER
JONI MITCHELL
SLY &
THE FAMILY STONE
CAT MOTHER
TINY TIM   FREE
JOHN SEBASTIAN
EMERSON,
LAKE & PALMER
MUNGO JERRY
SPIRIT   MILES DAVIS

SUNDAY 30th
JIMI HENDRIX
EXPERIENCE
JOAN BAEZ
DONOVAN
& OPEN ROAD
LEONARD COHEN
& THE ARMY
RICHIE HAVENS
MOODY BLUES
PENTANGLE
GOOD NEWS
RALPH McTELL

SPECIAL GUESTS
JETHRO TULL

learned a very important lesson on that first day. On the first take of "Miles Runs the Voodoo Down," I was playing my Tony Williams stuff, trying to impress Miles. It sounded great but that's not what he wanted. He came over to me and he said, "You ain't gettin' the chicken . . ." He wanted a real simple thing. So Don Alias said, "Miles, I got a beat." He played this—tuh, tuh, oom. And I said, "Awww man, I cannot believe this because I could have played *that*!" But I wasn't thinking that way. I ended up playing percussion on the tune.

I was so despondent. When I was packing up my stuff and Miles came to me. "Don't worry about it. Be here tomorrow at ten o'clock." So the next day we did "Spanish Key" and I was *in* it. I knew what I had to do—I had a totally newfound perspective. So "Spanish Key" is my favorite track.

Man, did *Bitches Brew* have an impact. Just look at that album cover man—it's amazing—and that music? I don't think there could be a better visual description of that music than that cover. Even today, you look at the album and say, "Whoooaaa!"

I remember people would say, "You made a record with Miles Davis—what's the name of it?" I'd say, "*Bitches Brew*." "*Witches Brew*?" "No, I said, *Bitches Brew*." "Oh, Witches *Brew*." "No, *BITCHES BREW!*"

OPPOSITE: Poster, Isle of Wight Festival, August 28–30, 1970.

ABOVE: Handbill, Fillmore West, San Francisco, California, October 15–19, 1970.

RIGHT: Poster, Fillmore West, San Francisco, California, May 6–9, 1971.

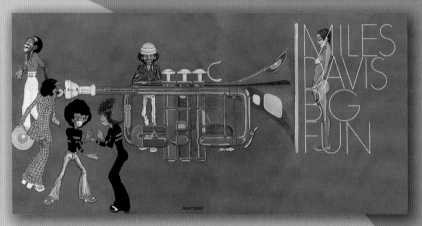

"It was with On the Corner *and* Big Fun *that I really made an effort to get my music over to young black people. They are the ones who buy records and come to concerts, and I had started thinking about building a new audience for the future. I already had gotten a lot of young white people coming to my concerts after* Bitches Brew *and so I thought it would be good if I could get all these young people together listening to my music and digging the groove."*

—Miles Davis, *Miles: The Autobiography*, 1989

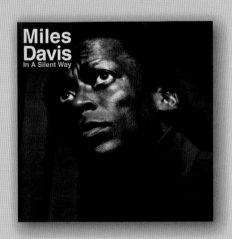

Poster and program, Ann Arbor Blues and Jazz Festival, Ann Arbor, Michigan,
September 8–10, 1971.

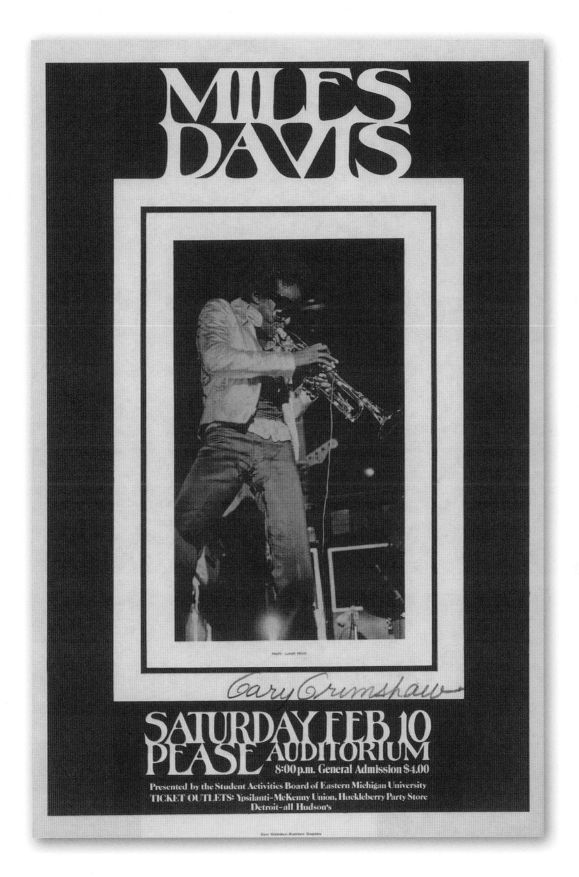

OPPOSITE: Miles, circa 1972. *Leni Sinclair/Michael Ochs Archives/Getty Images*

ABOVE: Handbill, Pease Auditorium, Ypsilanti, Michigan, February 10, 1973. *Designer: Gary Grimshaw*

Poster, Paramount Northwest, Portland, Oregon, April 4, 1973.

Chick Corea, Miles, and Dave Holland play at Ronnie Scott's jazz club in London for the BBC "Jazz Scene" TV show on November 2, 1969. *David Redfern/Redferns/ Getty Images*

Miles and drummer
James Foreman on stage
at Olympia Hall, Paris, on
July 11, 1973. *Alain Dejean/
Sygma/Corbis*

MILES GOES ACOUSTIC

by KARL HAGSTROM MILLER

KARL HAGSTROM MILLER is associate professor of History at the University of Texas in Austin. He is the author of *Segregating Sound: Inventing Folk and Pop Music in the Age of Jim Crow*.

L isten. Miles Davis enjoyed a long career of making music. There are dozens of doors into his body of work and each offers a different way of hearing. Where you enter can shape what you hear. This is a story of my introduction to the music of Miles Davis. It is personal. All such stories are.

Born in 1968, I came late to Miles Davis' acoustic jazz. The trumpeter cut *Bitches Brew* and *A Tribute to Jack Johnson* when I was in diapers. He seized upon the sounds of loud electric instruments that could vibrate your bones as well as your mind, and he never looked back. Much has been made about Miles going electric. The move stands as perhaps the most radical break in a long career of shape shifting and reinvention. Love it or hate it—and there are plenty of voices on either side of that equation—Miles' electric era is most often approached as heir to his groundbreaking acoustic music. Be it an extension or a rejection, progression or regression, the electric music came later.

Many fans at the time could not hear the new output without their familiarity with his earlier work coloring their perception of the music. By accident of birth, I had the opposite experience. In the history of my own listening, Miles never went electric. He went acoustic.

I first encountered Miles Davis at a tender age, when I pulled my father's pristine copy of *Bitches Brew* from the back of his record collection. An amateur trumpeter and a fan of Miles' Fifties sides, my father bought the record on faith but could not relate to what he heard. The album got buried after a cursory listen. I had a similar reaction. The music scared the hell out of me. The swirling rhythms, dark tonalities, and startling jump cuts sent me scurrying back to the comfort of Top 40 radio.

"I was using the wah-wah on my trumpet all the time so I could get closer to that voice Jimi [Hendrix] had when he used a wah-wah on his guitar. I had always played trumpet like a guitar and the wah-wah just made the sound closer."

—Miles Davis, *Miles: The Autobiography*, 1989

It was not until Miles returned from his retirement in 1981 that I began listening to him in earnest. During my teenage years, as I grew into a music fan and fledgling player, Miles' latest albums became go-to resources. I did not care that *Downbeat* critics didn't really dig the records or that they constantly compared them to older music I had not heard. In fact, I did not at first hear Miles as part of the history of jazz. What did I know about the history of jazz? I heard his new albums in relation to the rest of the music around me. Miles' records took many of the things I loved about music and made them better.

OPPOSITE: Miles blows his horn for the Montreux Jazz Festival, Montreux, Switzerland, on July 1, 1973. *David Warner Ellis/Redferns*

Advertisement, Carnegie Hall, New York City, March 30, 1974.

Take *We Want Miles*, the 1981 live album featuring Davis backed by bassist Marcus Miller, drummer Al Foster, saxophonist Bill Evans, and shred guitarist Mike Stern. In the early Eighties, my two favorite bands were Chic and Van Halen. Nile Rodgers' disco juggernaut was a groove machine. Hits like "Le Freak" were tight and exacting with an almost inhuman sheen. Eddie Van Halen was loose and joyfully sloppy in his unhinged guitar virtuosity. And his band, unlike so many hard rock units, could really swing. I came across *We Want Miles* in a used record store a few years after its release. It cracked my musical universe wide open.

Here was the Chic groove but with more open space, silence, and risk. "Jeanne Pierre" and "Back Seat Betty" were built around sparse bass riffs. But unlike "Le Freak" or "Good Times," the players improvised off of each other. There was never any doubt that Chic bassist Bernard Edwards was going to nail the repetitive groove each time around. It was delicious clockwork. Marcus Miller, on the other hand, made the groove breathe. He played with it. Toyed with it. Took it out, made it disappear, then brought it back hard. It was an unlikely miracle every time he made it back to the one. I was on the edge of my seat.

Then Stern dropped his syncopated rhythm work and hit the distortion pedal. The opening gesture of his guitar solo on "Jean Pierre" still gives me chills. Broad whammy-bar dives over a delicate groove: it was like Grand Funk Railroad dropping in on a dinner party. He then moved step by step, phrase by phrase, into deeper melodic waters. Stern later explained that Miles wanted him to play like Hendrix, but I heard it as pure Van Halen. Stern offered Eddie's tone combined with bop's harmonic sophistication. I was hooked. I set aside my previous obsessions and started looking for more Miles.

OPPOSITE: Poster, Carnegie Hall, New York City, March 3, 1974.

Star People intensified the *We Want Miles* formula with more rhythmic density. Al Foster's drum groove on "Come and Get It" sounded like Van Halen's "Hot for Teacher" flying off a cliff. *Decoy* turned dark and brooding with Stern's exclamatory phrasing replaced by John Scofield's diminished-scale mumblings. *Tutu* re-imagined *Dirty Mind*-era Prince. Critics decried the mechanical backing tracks, but I heard Miles and Marcus Miller revealing the ghosts in the machine. Miles' tender muted trumpet stood in for Prince's falsetto, and Miller replaced the sequencer with the subtle feel of live instruments even as the cuts "Tutu" and "Splatch" replicated the sampled orchestral hit of Afrika Bambaataa's "Planet Rock" and other early hip hop tracks. Miles forced me to hear the music of the day with new ears. I could never go back.

Tracking down the work of his collaborators—Miller, Scofield, Stern, Branford Marsalis, Daryl Jones, and, of course, Gil Evans—provided some of my first exposure to the deep rivers of jazz history. Branford Marsalis took me to New Orleans. Jones took me to Sting, the Police, and, eventually, the punk jazz of the Knitting Factory. Sco's early work led me to bassist Steve Swallow, who led me to Carla Bley, who led me to the Jazz Composer's Orchestra, Cecil Taylor, and the interrelationship between Duke Ellington and free jazz. I came to know Gil Evans as an old man whose wrinkled clothes and Native American headgear bespoke deranged tenured professor more than jazz titan. But his invigorating live albums from the New York jazz club Sweet Basil's erased the distance between Jimi Hendrix and Charles Mingus—who would soon become one of my personal favorites.

I also came to love and appreciate Miles' acoustic era masterpieces, from the aching minimalism of *Kind of Blue* to the lush maximalism of his work with Gil Evans. I was dazzled by the light gentility of his first great quintet featuring John Coltrane and Red Garland. I hung on every note as his Sixties quartet with Tony Williams transformed tunes from the American songbook into twenty-minute excursions into free improvisation. More than any other musician, Miles Davis became my guide through the history of postwar jazz.

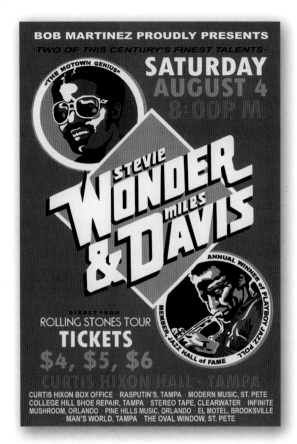

Poster, Curtis Hixon Hall, Tampa, Florida, August 4, 1973.

I inevitably heard the acoustic material as extensions and elaborations of the Eighties era music I already knew. When I listen to his Prestige recording of "When I Fall in Love" or "If I Were a Bell," I still hear the faint echoes of his 1985 cover of Cindy Lauper's "Time After Time." Each features his timid muted trumpet. Meaning emerges not from how he hits a note but from how he misses it. His fragility and vulnerability are revealed through the assured articulation of his backing musicians. At the time, his melodic slurs were derided as evidence of his lack of technique. After encountering his later style on Jack Johnson and other albums from the Seventies—full of smears, bends, and indeterminate pitches—his earlier works sound like case studies in restraint. His bum notes sound less like mistakes than evidence of a mature style yearning to break free.

The methodical, spacious "Nefertiti" from 1967 evokes the tension, drama, and feather-light groove of "That's Right" off of Miles' 1983 album *Decoy*. Each is slow and meticulous, focusing the ear on the twists and turns of each phrase, the subtle contour of each note. The smooth, chrome sonorities of the brass on *Birth of the Cool* echo the synthetic timbres of Tutu. And, I have to admit, I can't listen to his bebop work with Charlie Parker on cuts such as "Ornithology" or "Scrapple from the Apple" without hearing the uneven, off-kilter phrasing and rhythmic intensity of "You're Under Arrest," the killer title cut from the 1986 album best known for the cheesy photo of Miles posing with a toy gun.

I am not saying this is the best way to hear the music of Miles Davis. I'm not even saying that it is a good way. But it is all I've got.

The brilliant ethnomusicologist Steven Feld has argued that every listener carries in his or her head a unique collection of musical memories. Everything we have heard is bouncing around in our heads, and my collection is necessarily different than yours. Listeners encountering a new piece of music constantly compare what they are hearing to the music they already know. Consciously or not, the brain continually notes what is familiar and what is strange about the new sounds. The pleasure of listening to music, Feld insists, comes not from identifying one true or overriding meaning of the music at hand. The pleasure comes from the high-speed flittering of the brain as the music—moment by moment—confirms and upends the expectations we have built out of a lifetime of listening. What we have heard shapes what we hear.

One's listening history rarely corresponds to musicians' histories of making the music in the first place. The two follow different trails and separate logics. Every so often, however, they can cross paths. On a balmy summer night in 1991, Miles Davis took the stage at the Montreux Jazz Festival and did something many believed he would never do. He looked back. Musical innovation had been one of the few constants during his long, restless career reaching from bebop to hip hop. He regularly showed disinterest, if not disdain, for his earlier work. It was yesterday's news. He had his eyes on the future.

Yet on this one night, just a few months before his death at the age of 65, Miles Davis returned to some of his oldest and most celebrated music. The concert featured selections from his work with arranger Gil Evans: *The Birth of the Cool, Miles Ahead, Porgy and Bess, and Sketches of Spain*. His trademark trumpet floated atop the lush harmonies provided by several rows of brass and woodwind players. Davis, the jazz icon who for the past two decades had led bands full of loud and funky electric instruments, who had taught me how to hear and had led me down through music history, was back in front of a traditional jazz orchestra. The crowd was ecstatic. Conductor Quincy Jones was all smiles. Music once relegated to memories became manifest. Miles went acoustic.

OPPOSITE: Miles waits to go on stage at the Newport Jazz Festival on July 4, 1969. *David Redfern/Redferns/Getty Images*

7

Hiatus and Recovery

1975–1985

Miles blows at the 1985 North Sea
Jazz Festival in the Netherlands.
Eugene Maynard/Redferns/Getty Images

IN EARLY 1975, MILES TOURED JAPAN. Ill with pneumonia and a bleeding stomach ulcer, he medicated himself with alcohol, codeine, and morphine, his health growing ever more fragile. These concerts, the twilight of an idol, found Miles leading a band playing music so bleak and airless that it alienated many who came along. On February 1, Miles played two sets—in the afternoon and evening—at the Festival Hall in Osaka. Teo Macero was on hand to record these concerts, which Columbia would later issue (initially only in Japan) as the *Pangaea* and *Agharta* albums. Listening to the recordings, one hears Miles' trumpet occasionally penetrating the dense, wah-wah–driven rumble created by the band and there, even in pain, even drugged and drunk, the old master still blew his blues.

Back in the United States, Miles continued to tour but, on several occasions, needed to be hospitalized. After playing the Newport Jazz Festival in July 1975, he cancelled all further concerts and retreated to the shadows of his New York house. Visitors found him confined to bed, and there he would stay for the rest of the decade.

What caused Miles Davis to stop doing that thing most precious to him, making music? Depression, some have suggested, although Miles always denied it. Boredom was his answer. Exhaustion, suggested Gil Evans. He had been working in the public eye for almost thirty years and, as his health failed and the public ignored the new albums, perhaps Miles felt it prescient to conserve whatever energies he had left. Not that he looked after himself—life as a recluse involved shocking levels of self-degradation: chain-smoking cigarettes, guzzling cognac and beer, snorting copious amounts of cocaine, injecting drugs, dosing himself with sleeping pills, barely eating—a jazz vampire.

Lost in his addictions, Miles' house became a gathering place for dealers and hangers-on, a party—if that is the right word—always underway, a huge TV blaring out noise 24/7, the Manhattan madhouse. Admirers and old friends continued to drop in, but Miles withdrew into solipsism. Lovers came and went while he dedicated his creative energies to directing orgies, his physical frailty reducing him to an impotent voyeur. By late 1976, disco and funk, heavy metal and punk, were the big black and white music forms and none of them owed much to jazz. For the first time in his long career, Miles Davis found himself irrelevant. Rumors spread about "Miles the Recluse" and many wondered if he would ever emerge to make music again.

Not that this stopped those who loved his music from listening to it and debating the albums he had released across the 1970s. To fuel such interest, several Miles concert recordings were issued—three such sets in 1977 alone. These were almost all mid 1970s concerts and often consisted of Miles leading bands that jammed on wah-wah guitar riffs borrowed from Curtis Mayfield and Isaac Hayes hits. It was musical entropy.

Lester Bangs, the young critic who had written so presciently on *In a Silent Way*, wrote a furious, polemical essay on Miles in 1976. In it he dismissed almost all Davis' post-*Jack Johnson* recordings, declaring himself "obsessed, simply because he is Miles, one of the greatest musicians who ever lived, and when a giant gets cancer of the soul you have to weep or at least ask for a medical inquiry." Bangs suggested Miles should have called one of his recent albums *Kind of Grim* yet eloquently praised Miles' greatest recordings— "make no mistake, Miles understands pain—and he will pry it out of your soul's very core when he hits his supreme note and you happen, coincidentally, to be a bit of an open emotional wound at that moment yourself." Bangs noted how the recent albums indicate "that something was wrong with progenitor, that he was not indulging himself or tapped out or merely confused. That he was sick of soul."

Sick of soul is an apt description for Miles Davis in the late 1970s. Suffering bursitis of the wrists and shoulders, a disintegrating hip joint, toothache, stomach ulcers, and insomnia, he medicated himself with insane levels of drugs, both prescription and illegal. At one point he came close to having his left leg amputated, having constantly injected into a vein until it became ulcerated and dangerously inflamed. His two eldest sons both emulated their father's drug addictions, yet he offered them no compassion, instead rejecting both as "failures." Giving interviews during the 1980s, Miles refused to display contrition for this wasted era, instead boasting that he was "just having a good time." But those who witnessed him during these lost years suggest that nothing passed but time, and none of it was good. Old friends failed to penetrate Miles' desperate lethargy until Cicely Tyson reappeared.

In 1979, British musician Paul Buckmaster visited Miles and found the power at Davis' house cut off due to non-payment of bills. Buckmaster called Miles' sister, Dorothy, who arrived and, shocked at the squalor, rang Tyson, the actress having stayed in contact with Davis since their relationship ended. Tyson threw herself into saving Miles. She evicted the hangers-on, hired exterminators and cleaners, got an acupuncturist to work on the trumpeter, and began coaxing him out of his poisonous addictions.

Dorothy's son Vince Wilburn began visiting and played Uncle Miles tapes of his jazz-funk band. This rekindled Davis' interest in music and he convinced Columbia to book studio time for Vince's band and himself. Columbia—who had kept Miles on salary—were excited about getting new Miles recordings and financed the studio sessions. At the initial sessions, Miles found himself unable to play the trumpet—a five-year layoff had robbed him of his skills and his embouchure had withered. Humiliated, the world's foremost jazz musician found himself forced to practice playing trumpet for the first time in decades.

OPPOSITE: Miles on stage at the Avery Fisher Hall in New York City's Lincoln Centre in July 1975. *David Redfern/Redferns/Getty Images*

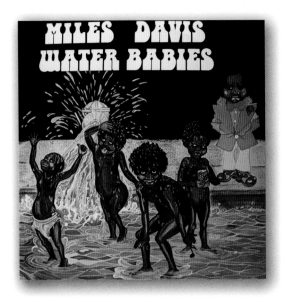

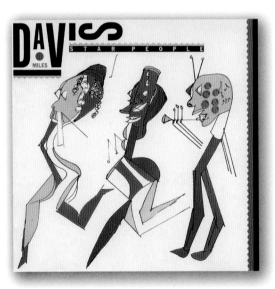

As Miles found his musical chops again, Teo Macero got back in the producer's seat, Gil Evans came in to help with arrangements, and top young musicians were hired, including bassist Marcus Miller. The resulting album *The Man with the Horn* finds Miles playing feebly over uninspired jazz-funk. Still, Miles' five-year absence had only served to increase his earning power as a live performer, and while he remained frail, the concert halls were packed with adoring audiences. Jazz critic Stanley Crouch derided Miles' New York concert as "an obvious con job in its obvious manipulation of the audience's eagerness to like whatever he did" before adding "but his homemade post-bebop sound is still more moving than anything I've heard on trumpet since Clifford Brown."

Cannonball Adderley suffered a fatal stroke in 1975, Charlie Mingus died in 1979, and Bill Evans passed in 1980. The ranks of the core musicians Miles had created modern jazz alongside were thinning, and Miles found himself missing his old comrades. That he had survived when so many of his contemporaries had fallen increased his legend and ensured he was in ever greater demand.

In 1981, Davis married Cicely Tyson at a ceremony hosted by Bill Cosby. Tyson kept vigilant watch on Miles, but when she went to film in Africa, he returned to old habits and suffered a minor stroke. Again, Tyson nursed him, and Miles finally dedicated himself to a strict drug- and alcohol-free existence. The onset of diabetes meant his doctor gave him a "life or death" option—including no sex for six months, to which Davis complied.

The 1982 live-in-concert double album *We Want Miles*, drawn from three dates of his comeback tour, sold well and won a Grammy for Best Jazz Instrumental Performance by a Soloist. That the Miles being celebrated appeared a pale shadow of the musician who once played with such fire and grace did not attract much comment—America loves a survivor. Miles, now moving in Tyson's showbiz world, became a celebrity who advertised scooters and played a pimp on the television show "Miami Vice."

The 1983 album *Star People* found Miles, Teo Macero, and Gil Evans working closely together for the last time. But the old magic failed to surface and the album received little attention. *Decoy* from 1984, Miles' first self-produced album, was a poor attempt at creating pop funk and won him the worst reviews of his career. Disinterested in the recording process, Miles left much of the work to keyboardist Robert Irving III, and Irving proved to be no Macero.

Poster, Porte de Pantin, Paris, April 12–13, 1983.

> *"Fewer and fewer black musicians were playing jazz and I could see why, because jazz was becoming the music of the museum. A lot of musicians and critics are at fault for letting it happen. No one wants to be dead before their time, you know, when they're twenty-one, and that's what was going to happen to someone who went into jazz."*
>
> **—Miles Davis, *Miles: The Autobiography*, 1989**

Miles refused to perform his now-classic recordings, stating he had to keep looking forward rather than back. When a promoter approached him to tour with Herbie Hancock, Wayne Shorter, and Ron Carter, Miles declined. Jazz, he said, was like an old man dying in bed, and he didn't want to be associated with death.

Still, he displayed only a cursory interest in making new music: *Decoy* suggested a palpable contempt for his audience. Interviewers were constantly told by the trumpeter that he was currently making the best music of his life, but to anyone paying attention it was clear that Miles now appeared more interested in creating paintings than music, his large canvases—influenced by Picasso and Basquiat—being exhibited at reputable dealer galleries.

Miles next announced he wanted to record an album of covers of contemporary pop hits. Work began, but 1985's *You're Under Arrest* ended up consisting of largely original material with only Toto's "Human Nature" and Cyndi Lauper's "Time After Time" remaining. *Under Arrest* is slick jazz-funk immediately dated by its over-reliance on synthesizers, yet it stands as the one Miles album from the 1980s that reflects the trumpeter's personality. The opening tune, "One Phone Call/Street Scenes," starts with the sound of cocaine being snorted, and a certain bleak humor pervades its entirety.

Invited to Denmark to receive the Léonie Sonning Music Award in December 1984, Miles was impressed by "Aura," a contemporary classical suite composed for the event by Palle Mikkelborg. In January, Miles returned to Denmark to record some of "Aura" only to find Columbia unenthusiastic about issuing the recordings. *Aura* is an odd mix of New Age mood muzak and jazz funk, but Miles found it inspiring, and throughout he blows with concentration and finesse. Columbia finally released *Aura* in 1989. But by then Miles was happily ensconced at Warner Brothers and more rich and famous than at any time since *Bitches Brew*.

Poster, Palais des Sports, Bordeaux, France, April 22, 1983.

Poster, Bercy Jazz Non Stop, Paris, November 6, 1984.

MILES *AND* WOMEN

by NALINI JONES

NALINI JONES is the author of the acclaimed short story collection *What You Call Winter*. Her work has appeared in the *Ontario Review*, *Glimmer Train*, *Dogwood*, and *Creative Nonfiction*.

Paris, 1970: my father, who has spent his life working for the jazz impresario George Wein, introduced Miles Davis to my mother for the first time. Miles lifted her fingers as if to simply kiss them, then slowly licked her arm from hand to elbow. Dad said nothing but firmly removed my mother's arm, then my mother, from the scene.

As a kid, I prickled with discomfort whenever I heard this story. As I grew older, working backstage at festivals, lugging tubs of ice, meeting shuttle vans, dispensing passes, I learned how to reconcile foolish or just plain lousy behavior offstage, with beautiful music onstage. I learned that Miles was being Miles. His code was not other people's code.

But pettiness is not the same as cruelty; eccentricity is not the same as capricious abuse. "Miles being Miles" could refer to charming walks along the Seine in 1949 with Juliette Gréco, "the first woman," he wrote in his autobiography, "that I loved as an equal human being." Or it could refer to "the whole stable of bitches" Miles pimped two years later, during the worst years of his heroin abuse and while in a common-law relationship with the mother of his first three children. His idea of a joke could range from the tender riddles he shared with his companion Jo Gelbard in the late-1980s, to the chilling laugh he shared with police officers summoned by his third wife, Cicely Tyson, to investigate a call of domestic violence in 1985. "Well, if she's beating my ass you gonna come with your guns ready, too?"

The man who licked my mother's arm was as complicated as that gesture has come to seem, as variable as the women he loved. "I didn't know what to do," my mother said when I asked why she didn't just pull away. She may as well have been responding to a larger question: what do we do with an artist of such stark and disturbing contradictions?

In 1990, a year before Miles Davis' death, Pearl Cleage raised this question with reluctance and devastating power in her watershed essay, "Mad at Miles." She opened describing her ambivalence: Miles Davis was not just a brilliant musician and composer but an iconic cultural figure, hailed by many African Americans as a leader. Cleage knew that questioning him would be regarded as a betrayal of her community. And she had to reckon with her own deep personal appreciation of his music. She wrote of "listening to Miles Davis play me into the next phase of my life," and how her "seduction ritual" became: "Chill the wine. Light the candles. Put on a little early Miles."

"I confess," Cleage wrote, "I spent many memorable evenings sending messages of great personal passion through the intricate improvisations of *Kind of Blue . . .*" "*But I didn't know then*," she added in italics—in a relentless refrain through the essay—"*he was guilty of self-confessed violent crimes against women such that we ought to break his records, burn his tapes, and scratch up his CDs until he acknowledges and apologizes and agrees to rethink his position on The Woman Question.*"

Cleage wasn't angry just because Miles mistreated women; she was angry because his actions deprived her of his music. In her essay, she tries to find a way out, a way to continue to listen to Miles, feeling what she felt and then knowing what she knows. "But that didn't work. I kept thinking about Cicely Tyson, hiding in the basement of her house" after Miles "slapped the shit out of her." Cleage wonders "if thinking about his genius made [Tyson] less frightened and humiliated."

Miles plays for the Nice Jazz Festival, Nice, France, in July 1985. *David Redfern/ Getty Images*

Miles, 1985. *Aaron Rapoport/Corbis*

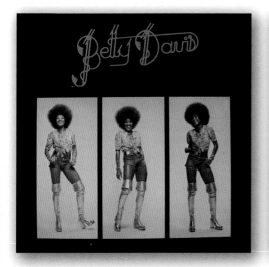 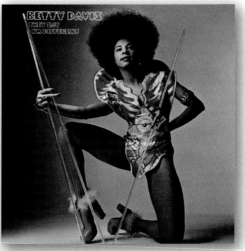 

Betty Davis, née Mabry, became Miles' second wife, introducing him to Jimi Hendrix and a new generation of rock 'n' roll that would dramatically influence Miles' own music going forward.

Miles' own defense serves as further indictment. In his autobiography, he laments the need to hit women—"I don't like that kind of feeling or doing that to a woman . . . but if you let it slide too many times . . . they're going to keep getting up in your face . . . pushing you and pushing you. Then you get mad and might hit them." In his recollection of the episode with Tyson that Cleage describes, Miles admits that "before I knew it I had slapped her again . . . she never did pull that kind of shit on me again."

Miles goes on to offer a host of diagnoses for such distressing pushiness—in the case of American black women, it's their lack of confidence, he decides, "because of their hair and the brainwashing this country has put on them." It's that they "see themselves as teachers or mothers when it comes to a man." If only they could be more like Japanese, Ethiopian, or Brazilian women, "who respect men and don't ever try acting like a man."

Yet women are essential to Miles Davis' music—viscerally, elegantly, spiritually, soulfully, sexually involved. They're not cowering in the basement; they're at the heart of his work. His first wife Frances Taylor drew him into the world of theater and dance, inspiring his recording *Porgy and Bess* and his explorations of African rhythms. In the 1960s, his second wife Betty Mabry rekindled his career by introducing Miles to Jimi Hendrix, Sly Stone, and other rock and soul artists whose music "helped point the way I was to go" on such ground-breaking albums as *In a Silent Way* and the explosive *Bitches Brew*. And Cicely Tyson was the woman who helped guide him back to health after he spent the late 1970s in a haze of drug addiction. The fierce pride he saw in her, "a kind of inner-burning fire," was an example and support—until it became a reason to slap her.

Miles could be charming when he chose; how else could he have drawn such remarkable women to him? He was capable of great warmth, and humor. He could rage on the phone with George's talent booker Marie St. Louis, then make her laugh a huge, wolfish laugh. He respected George's West Coast producer Darlene Chan because she stood up to him. He was capable of self-reflection: "I made a mistake when I broke up with her," he admitted about Frances Taylor. He was contradictory and he knew it. "I'm a Gemini and I can be real nice one minute and into something else the next."

Cleage doesn't claim to know the answer to the question of how to ultimately reconcile such opposites—Miles with his music. Her essay ends with a series of urgent questions: "How can they hit us and still be our leaders? Our husbands? Our loves, our geniuses, our friends? And the answer is . . . they can't. *Can they*?"

What Cleage did know is that she could not listen to Miles anymore. She banned *Kind of Blue*. She refused to support the work of a man who beat women without apology.

I am listening to *Kind of Blue* as I write, because I have not thrown it away. I have not tossed out my James Brown albums, nor my books by V. S. Naipaul. If I had a Picasso, I would surely keep it. I've not investigated the lives of countless other artists whose acts of violence and misogyny may place their creations off-limits to some. I know an artist's genius cannot provide an excuse for violence and I know that Miles' acts cannot be redeemed by any number of tender ballads. It's a terrible irony that the man who was a fiery innovator in music could resort to such tired clichés in justifying his misdeeds.

Miles Davis is among the handful of musicians who have shown us that art can move beyond its time, beyond the hands and minds that formed it. In truly great music there's always a promise of transcendence; it is possible to hear the promise in Miles' music without any interest in his redemption.

MILES DAVIS IN THE RING: THE BOXER AS BLACK MALE HERO

by GERALD EARLY

Essayist and critic **GERALD EARLY** is the editor of *Miles Davis and American Culture* and *The Culture of Bruising: Essays on Prizefighting, Literature, and Modern American Culture*. He served as a consultant on Ken Burns' documentary film *Jazz* and is a regular commentator on National Public Radio's "Fresh Air."

"Boxing is like music."

—Miles Davis, 1970 *Down Beat* interview with Dan Morgenstern

In the United States, title fights make the front page of major newspapers. From the turn of the century to at least the 1980s, boxing was a major sport in the U.S., dubious in character because of its underworld connections and the damaging, remorseless results of its violence. But it also has that attractive sense of opposition, of competition, of how we imagine ideally how conflict should resolve itself, in an arena where the combatants fight one to one. There is something sternly moral about this.

The heavyweight champion—physically, the biggest of all—still stands as the king of kings. And by turn of the twentieth century boxing began to have black heavyweight champions. Boxing was the only major American professional sport that was integrated before World War II. Blacks had been champions of various weight divisions since the late nineteenth century, so many blacks followed the sport at least casually because of this. The greatness of black fighters reflected a kind of race pride, all the more so that most black fighters had to fight and defeated more than a few white fighters if they were to be champions.

Miles Davis "grew up loving boxing," according to his son Gregory's biography, *Dark Magus*. He was eleven years old when Joe Louis became only the second black heavyweight champion and an American icon in 1937, when he defeated the Cinderella Man, James Braddock, in eight rounds. Davis was twenty-five years old in 1951, and a rising professional jazz musician, when an over-the-hill Louis fought his last fight, an eight-round knockout at the hands of Rocky Marciano. In other words, Davis lived his adolescence and entered his young adult years having experienced the arc of Louis' career as one of the most prominent, nay, eminent black men of his age, a hero for millions of blacks not only in the U.S. but also around the world.

Louis was also a hero for white Americans as well, a symbol for the U.S. and democracy in 1938, in his second fight against Nazi champion Max Schmeling (Louis lost the first bout in 1936), where he knocked out the German in the first round. In short, Louis was not the first or the only "crossover" figure of Davis' youth but he was the most dramatic (after all, athletic competition is an obvious risk and has considerable pressure) and the most famous such figure, because he was a star athlete.

PALAIS DES CONGRES
T.D.M. présente
MILES DAVIS
PRIX 150 F
Lundi 31 Oct. 1983 à 21h
7 D07
Lundi 31 Oct. 1983 à 21h
№ 000989
Ce billet ne peut être ni repris, ni échangé.   SOLA PARIS

OPPOSITE: Miles performs at the Beacon Theatre, New York City, in April 1986.
Everett Collection/Alamy

Miles performs, circa 1984. *Jim Britt/Michael Ochs Archives/Getty Images*

As Davis noted in his autobiography, "[Louis] was every black person's hero—and a lot of white people's, too."

Davis' biographer Ian Carr writes that trumpeter Clark Terry, a St. Louisian—Davis was born across the river in Alton, Illinois, and cut his musical teeth playing in St. Louis—and a major influence on a youthful Davis, was "an excellent boxer and a close friend of Archie Moore," the Mongoose, who was also one of the great fighters of the post-World War II era.

Terry recalled his attraction to boxing as an adolescent in his autobiography: "I loved my new 'macho' image, and I wanted to learn more about fighting. So it made sense to me that I needed to go over to Kid's gym and learn from a pro. Didley went with me a few times, but he just couldn't dig it. When I got good enough to start boxing, I won a few fights, and I noticed how the girls were flirting with me more and more. I dug that. And the thrill of kicking ass gave me a

real rush. My muscles got tight, and I gained a reputation for being a winner. I started loving boxing almost as much as playing my horn, and I thought about becoming a professional."

Moore, too, was from St. Louis. As was Henry Armstrong, probably the most exciting boxer of the 1930s. The only other black men who could have impressed a young Miles Davis as much or more were jazz musicians.

Davis commented in a 1974 *Down Beat* interview, "I like it when a black boy says, 'Oohh! Man, there's Miles Davis.' Like they did with Joe Louis. . . . I would like for black people to look at me like Joe Louis." It is extraordinary that Davis did not say "Like they did with Duke Ellington," or "Like they did with Louis Armstrong." Or that he didn't say that he wanted black people to look up to him as they did Ellington or Basie, Ray Charles or James Brown. He does not mention a musician who has peerage of esteem among young blacks that he man with a certain cool veneer than Louis lacked, and a very stylish, cool boxer considered by most experts to have been the greatest boxer, pound-for-pound, in the history of the sport. Robinson had also spent some time in show business as a dancer when he retired from boxing in the early 1950s, only to return to the sport when his show biz career fizzled and he needed money.

Davis elaborates on Robinson as his inspiration for kicking his heroin habit in the early 1950s in his autobiography (p. 174). When Davis began training as a boxer in the 1950s, he sometimes worked out at the same New York gym as Robinson, who was an active professional fighter until 1965. "I really used to watch Ray, idolized him. When I told him one day that summer that he was the prime reason that I broke my heroin habit, he just smiled and laughed." (*Miles: The Autobiography*, p. 182) According to Davis' son Gregory, the trumpeter and Robinson "were buddies," who visited each other's homes from time to time. (*Dark Magus*, p. 116)

So, Robinson inspired Davis not only to clean himself but to train as a boxer in both Chicago and New York. Davis never fought beyond some sparring in the ring and largely used boxing as a form of exercise, something that most boxing trainers would prefer for fitness types not to do. It strikes them as reductionist and pointless. In a 1969 *Down Beat* interview Davis did about his boxing, he said the training "gives you a lot of strength. It's good for your wind. I mean, when I go to play something that I know is kind of impossible to play, I have that strength, that wind." In short, boxing represented for Davis a kind of physical virtue, a discipline that was, in its way, akin to music. Despite the obvious risk of a professional trumpeter boxing (one punch in the mouth might ruin his embouchure and his ability to make his livelihood forever), Davis rather thought boxing made him stronger as a jazz player, and made him "blacker," in some sense, as a man in that he connected with other strong black men.

What is interesting is that Robinson, who was an old Ellington–Basie–Lunceford type of jazz fan (the music he grew up with) much like novelists Ralph Ellison and Albert Murray, probably was not a fan of Davis' boxing tribute music. For Robinson, it probably would have been a bit too ultra-modern.

admires. He mentions the man that he himself so deeply admired when he was a boy, a prizefighter so good and so important that he raised the hopes and reflected the national character of his people. In a quest for black male heroism, nothing quite matches the mythical individuality, the moment-of-truth courage of the champion fighter.

To be sure, at the time of the interview, Davis made a major recording, a soundtrack to a documentary about turn-of-the-century heavyweight Jack Johnson, the first black heavyweight champion and a controversial public figure, largely because of his very public relationships with white women at a time when interracial sex between black men and white women was not only discouraged but in many parts of the country illegal and violently suppressed. (The documentary, produced by two men who were to become Mike Tyson's managers, Jim Jacobs and Bill Cayton, is difficult to find.)

The soundtrack album—adeptly edited by Davis producer Teo Macero—was probably the most perfect marriage of jazz and rock in the annals of American popular music. It was made between February 18 and June 4, 1970. Howard Sackler's play, *The Great White Hope*, a fictionalized account of Johnson's career, had opened on Broadway in 1967, to a very successful run and Martin Ritt's film version was released in 1970 just a few months after Davis' soundtrack album. So, Jack Johnson was very much in the cultural air of the period. Ali's return in boxing in the fall of 1970, around the time of the *White Hope* film, after a three-and-one-half year enforced layoff because of his opposition to the Vietnam War and the draft, made boxing a major news story and much part of the culture of the time.

In the 1974 interview, Davis continued his tribute to boxers, saying "Sugar Ray Robinson inspired me, and he made me kick a habit. I said, 'If that mother can win all those fights, I sure can break this motherfuckin' habit.' " It is not surprising that Robinson would have become a particular hero to Davis: Robinson—a welterweight and middleweight (professional fighting weight between 140 and 160 pounds) was a smaller man than Louis, closer in stature to Davis, who was also enamored of a lesser known welterweight named Johnny Bratton; Robinson was dark-skinned like Davis, was a very stylish

8

Tutu
and Farewell

Miles, 1989. *Michel Comte/Corbis Outline*

***YOU'RE UNDER ARREST* GAVE MILES A TASTE** of mainstream success with "Time After Time" and "Human Nature" getting played on smooth jazz and adult-oriented pop radio stations. From bebop to pop rock, Davis had embraced and tangled with a wide variety of musical styles across almost forty years as a professional musician. Yet no matter how often he changed his sidemen, one thing remained constant in his music: Miles' trumpet playing, its blue tone and direct, emotional character.

From playing the standards of his youth to those of 1980s pop, Miles appeared to have come full circle (and both "Time After Time" and "Human Nature" would remain in his live set right up to the end). Yet he remained restless, hungry now not for new musical challenges but greater commercial rewards. Once seen as an icon of African American militancy, Davis now made it clear only money mattered. In interviews he dismissed jazz as "dead" and praised Prince and Michael Jackson, wanting their mass audiences (and the huge wealth they generated). That Miles had no desire to fight the power is reflected in his autobiography's funniest—if bile-filled—passage: he and Cicely Tyson are invited to Ronald Reagan's White House for an event honoring Ray Charles. Twice elderly white women, trying to be friendly, patronize Davis, so receive hectoring replies in return. Yet to President Reagan, Miles reacted differently. Reagan was an arch-conservative who, whilst Governor of California, worked towards bringing down the Black Panthers and refused to let Mohammed Ali box in the Golden State, and, as President, had made it clear he disliked the idea of Martin Luther King Jr.'s birthday becoming a national holiday and supported South Africa's apartheid regime. To Reagan, Miles genuflects with surprising affection.

Poster, Belga Jazz Festival, Antwerp, Belgium, October 18, 1987.

OPPOSITE: Miles plays the New Orleans Jazz Festival, Spring 1986. *David Redfern/ Getty Images*

In Reagan's America money ruled, and Miles, who loved to shop and surrounded himself with luxury goods and expensive cars, agreed. But to participate fully he needed greater income. Thus his surprising shift to Warner Brothers in 1985. Surprising, that is, to Columbia, who had stood by Miles through the fat and lean years. Warners offered Davis a considerable signing fee—if Miles had chosen to negotiate with Columbia it is possible they might have matched the offer (and the Warner deal found Davis signing over his entire publishing). But Miles was not happy with Columbia's promotion of newcomer Wynton Marsalis, and furious when Columbia Jazz's head honcho George Butler dared suggest that he, the mighty Miles, call Wynton and wish him happy birthday. The Miles–Wynton feud was latched onto by a media who love a celebrity spat, especially one involving the grand old man of modern jazz and the young contender. Wynton, from a noted New Orleans family of musicians, considered jazz America's classical music and derided much of the music marketed as jazz from the late 1960s onwards—free jazz, jazz fusion, jazz funk, smooth jazz, etc.—as "not jazz." Of Miles, whose

recordings from the late 1940s through to the late 1960s Marsalis admired, he expressed disbelief that the master had so lost his way. These criticisms stung Miles—long used to being number one—especially coming from a young, black jazz trumpeter with brilliant technique and a high profile. The low point of their conflict came in September 1986 when both musicians found themselves booked at the Vancouver Festival. Wynton walked on stage carrying his trumpet during Miles' set and Miles, rather than inviting Marsalis to sit in or challenging him to a cutting contest, stopped his band and insisted they would not play until Marsalis got off his stage. Miles, formerly a reluctant interviewee, now embraced the media to speak with vitriol about Wynton.

Tutu, Miles' 1986 Warners debut, featured a striking, Irving Penn cover portrait of Davis. It also featured a slick, synthesized pop-funk sound. *Tutu* is not the album Miles initially hoped to issue. Working with producer Randy Hall, and calling on help from the likes of Prince, Chaka Khan, and Al Jarreau, he had started recording what was to be called *Rubberband*. Tommy LiPuma, head honcho of Warners' jazz

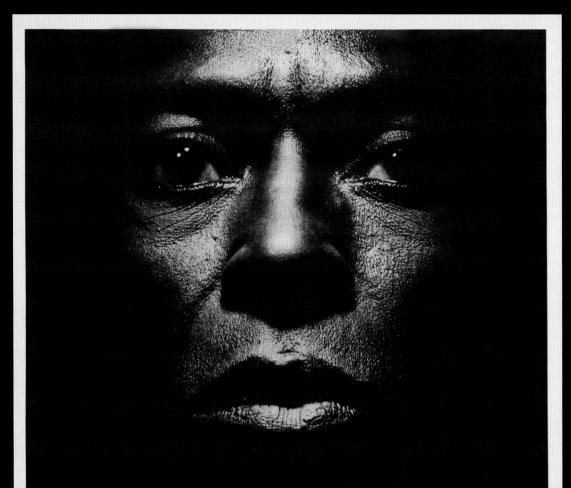

MILES DAVIS
IN CONCERT

Montag
23. 11. '87
Einlaß 19 Uhr, Beginn 20 Uhr

MUSIC HALL
jovel
Münster, Grevener Str. 91

Vorverkaufsstellen: Münster: Elpi, Cha Cha, Leeze, L'Hippopotame, Jörgs CD Forum · Osnabrück: Radio Deutsch
Coesfeld: Schallplattentruhe · Steinfurt: Reisebüro Frie · Detmold: Strathmann · Dortmund: live station · Rheine:
Ohrwurm · Hagen und Bochum: ELPI · Hamm, Gronau: CD Forum
Tel. Kartenservice: 0251/797477 · 0541/83019

Poster, Music Hall Jovel, Munster, Germany, November 23, 1987.

division, buried the *Rubberband* sessions, determining that Miles on Warners would answer to his corporate vision. When Marcus Miller, the gifted bassist who had played on Miles' first two comeback albums and produced several Luther Vandross hits, called to ask if LiPuma was interested in hearing material he had composed with the possibility of Miles recording it, Tommy assented.

Miller presented LiPuma with several demos of lightly funky, heavily synthesized music. LiPuma immediately told Miller to get Miles in to play trumpet over the recordings. Miller was surprised both at the size of the assignment—from mere bassist he was suddenly anointed composer and producer of Miles Davis!—and by LiPuma's declaration that no further musicians were needed. Miles came in and blew over Miller's airless instrumentals, insisting only that they record a version of "Perfect Way," a pop song whose melody appealed to Miles. LiPuma—credited as co-producer—then added George Duke's "Backyard Ritual," the only song he considered worth salvaging from the *Rubberband* sessions, and oversaw a handful of overdubs. Naming the album after South Africa's Archbishop Desmond Tutu—the anti-apartheid movement's most voluble figurehead—was a canny move on LiPuma's part

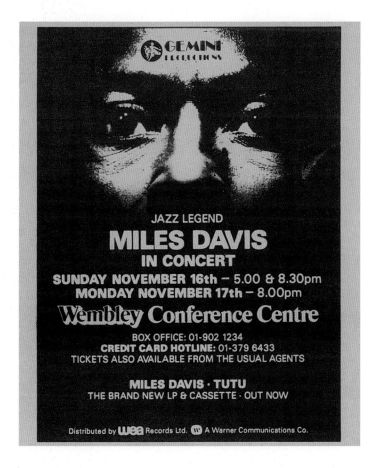

Advertisement, Wembley Conference Centre, London, November 16–17, 1986.

as it lent Miles a hip political status. Warners heavily promoted *Tutu*, and the album received good reviews and sold strongly. Miles went out on the road, and his touring band—featuring a succession of guitarists—played the material with a great deal more attack than found on *Tutu*.

Asked to write the soundtrack for Mary Lambert's movie *Siesta*, Miles agreed, then turned the project over to Miller. The film bombed and the soundtrack drew little attention, neither Miles nor Miller appearing to consider it anything more than an easy payday.

Drawing heavily on Prince's funk-rock sound, Miles led his young band around the world. He dressed in Japanese robes and played red and green trumpets with a microphone connected to the bell through which he would, at times, communicate with the audience. If his new music lacked the fierce edge of previous decades, Miles was a more expansive character, accommodating to media and gracious towards audiences. Yet something still raged within Miles. Repeated acts of violence finally drove Cicely Tyson away—she had dragged Miles out of addiction's fog and returned him to health, but Davis would boast in his autobiography of the beatings he dealt to Cicely while cruelly suggesting he never felt attracted to her. Gil Evans, the arranger who had been Miles' closest friend, died aged seventy-six in 1988. Miles mourned Gil's passing by withdrawing from making music and concentrating on painting. His new partner was Jo Gelbard, a painter and sculptor who had met Miles when they were neighbors in an exclusive Fifth Avenue apartment complex (Cicely Tyson had once punched Gelbard due to her suspicions).

The 1989 album *Amandla*—produced by Miller, LiPuma, and George Duke—mined a similar formula to *Tutu*, even down to using the Zulu word for "power" in the title. Miller contributed most of the material, with Duke providing one tune. This time, LiPuma allowed for a variety of jazz musicians to guest on sessions while Miles' painted self-portrait adorned the cover. *Amandla* is competent, if rather flat, and was received as such. During recording, Miles collapsed with bronchial pneumonia and, disregarding doctors' advice that he retire from touring, he returned to the road. The year 1989 also saw the publication of *Miles: The Autobiography*. As a memoir it is frustrating. Miles is often reluctant to discuss music making (*Kind of Blue* gets a single page that largely concentrates on Davis declaiming how he, not Bill Evans, created the album's music, while failing to mention how the sessions came together or what inspired the sublime solo in "So What"). He is parsimonious in the acknowledgement he gives to the musicians and producers he worked with; the most grievous being the little attention paid to Teo Macero's late-1960s efforts. Instead, the wizened legend is more content to boast about womanizing and drugging, and rant about race. But his droll wit, and the scorching comments on Charlie Parker and other noted jazz musicians, certainly offered an intimate glimpse of the men (and occasional female vocalist) who created modern jazz.

Poster, ICC Saal, Berlin, November, 3, 1987.

Miles, 1988. *Lynn Goldsmith/Corbis*

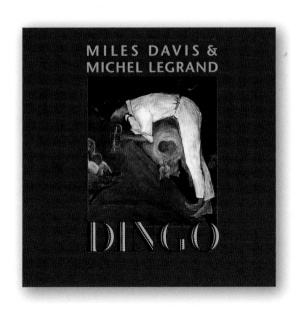

Finally, *Miles: The Autobiography* is illuminating in what Miles' rants reveal about the man: Angry, insecure and incapable of love, Davis constantly wants to portray himself as a tough guy, a badass. Yet genuine tough guys tend to avoid genuflecting to their celebrity buddies, and throughout the book Miles appears desperate for the approval from the more famous (he mentions Prince—who played little role in any part of his career, beyond a late mutual admiration society—more often and more affectionately than any and all of his four children). It soon emerged that Davis and co-author Quincy Troupe had based entire passages on Jack Chambers' two-volume biography of Miles, as Miles was seemingly incapable of recalling his own history.

In 1990, Miles appeared on two soundtracks—the odd Australian-French feature *Dingo* and the Dennis Hopper-directed crime thriller, *The Hot Spot*. Miles even agreed to act in *Dingo*, and his playing on the soundtrack (which he did not

"A lot of people tell me I have the mind of a boxer, that I think like a boxer, and I probably do. I guess that I am an aggressive person about things that are important to me, like when it comes to playing music or doing what I want to do."

—**Miles Davis, *Miles: The Autobiography*, 1989**

score) finds him in fine form. For *The Hot Spot*, celebrated soundtrack composer/producer Jack Nitzsche hired Miles alongside bluesmen Taj Mahal and John Lee Hooker, so creating a swampy soundtrack more memorable than the finished film. Miles also played on albums cut by Scritti Politti, Toto, Chaka Khan, Cameo, Marcus Miller, Kenny Garrett, and Shirley Horn, as well as Quincy Jones' star-laden *Back on the Block*. On the latter Miles found himself joining stars of jazz, soul, and rap—although he surely felt disappointed when the rapper Big Daddy Kane said "Who's Miles Davis?" when asked by Jones to rap a rhyme of praise for the trumpeter. Inspired by Jones' album, Miles began recording with rap producer Easy Mo Bee. Interrupting sessions to go on tour, he surprised everyone by agreeing to perform material he had once recorded with Gil Evans at Switzerland's Montreux Jazz Festival. For decades Davis had insisted he wasn't going back "to that old shit" but on July 8, 1991, he took the stage in front of an orchestra conducted by Quincy Jones to do just that. Miles, ever the pragmatist, replied when asked about this, "In the first place, they offered me a lot of money." Back in the United States, Miles played what would be his final-ever concert at the Hollywood Bowl on August 25. Not long after, he was hospitalized. A stroke then paralyzed him and he fell into a coma, lingering for several weeks before dying on September 28, 1991. Fulsome obituaries and tributes appeared around the world although Miles' ex-wives and children remained largely silent.

His jazz-rap album, *Doo-Bop*, was completed by using outtakes from the *Rubberband* recordings and won a 1992 Grammy—undeservedly, *Doo-Bop* being inconsequential Miles. Today dozens of Miles Davis' live albums documenting the trumpeter's entire career are available alongside "complete" sessions multi-CD box sets of *Bitches Brew*, *Jack Johnson*, and *In a Silent Way*. His music is remixed, sampled, imitated, debated, re-imagined, academicized, philosophized, and sold in every which way.

As was once writ about Bird—*Miles lives!*

ABOVE LEFT: Guitarist Foley (Joseph Foley McCreary) jams with Miles at the Pier on August 27, 1988. *Ebet Roberts/Redferns/Getty Images*

OPPOSITE: Miles, 1989. *Ebet Roberts/Redferns*

Miles performs—both on stage and superimposed on screen behind the band—at the North Sea Jazz Festival, the Hague, The Netherlands, in 1990. *Reuters/Corbis*

MILES *IN THE* *1980s*

by GREG TATE

Writer, musician, and producer **GREG TATE** was a staff writer for the *Village Voice* from 1987 through 2005. His work has appeared in the *New York Times*, the *Washington Post*, *Down Beat*, *JazzTimes*, and *Rolling Stone*. He is the author of *Everything But the Burden: What White People Are Taking From Black Culture,* among other titles.

First jazz album I ever copped was *In a Silent Way*. The year was 1972; the place, downtown Dayton, Ohio. Your boy strolls into some basement record haunt committed to buying a jazz album, any jazz album. He'd been mightily inspired after being consumed by LeRoi Jones' essay collection *Black Music*, transformed the kid from a Marvel comic book fan to Black musical superhero groupie. Who needs the Fantastic Four when you've got the Coltrane Quartet? My Dark Knight becomes Miles in an instant. Dewey's chiseled black-and-blue granite visage leaps off the wall to own a brother at hello.

People always say *Kind of Blue* is the best introduction to jazz, but *IASW* was my own portal into the hot. Well, that, and my second jazz purchase, *Thembi*—Pharaoh Sanders striking a mean pose somewhere between village priest and country preacher.

You can't talk about Miles in the 1970s and not talk about radical Black Music, radical Black Politics and radical Black Visual Style. It was the best and the worst of times in Black America depending on how your people were left standing after 1968's hundred-city riots and rebellions that had hollowed out urban America in retaliation for Dr. King's assassination. Black families led by militant middle-class aspirant, college-educated parents like my own fled the rotting urban core for 'burbs where American apartheid was now illegal thanks to the 1964 Civil Rights Act. In our case the move was to DC's "Gold Coast."

Soul Train was the upbeat reflection of our self-image back then. The ghetto-centric noir of Blaxploitation cinema provided a more grimy and melodramatic counterpoint. In 1971, Black popular music took on a much darker tinge and for some time afterwards that can be heard on Jimi Hendrix's posthumously released swansong *Band of Gypsys*, Gil Scott-Heron's *Small Talk at 125th and Lenox*; Marvin Gaye's *What's Going On*; Funkadelic's *Maggot Brain*; War's *The World is a Ghetto*; The O'Jays *Back Stabber*s; Earth, Wind & Fire's *Last Days and Time*; Labelle's *Pressure Cookin'* ; and Bob Marley and the Wailers' *Catch a Fire*. This was the soul music of a dream deferred.

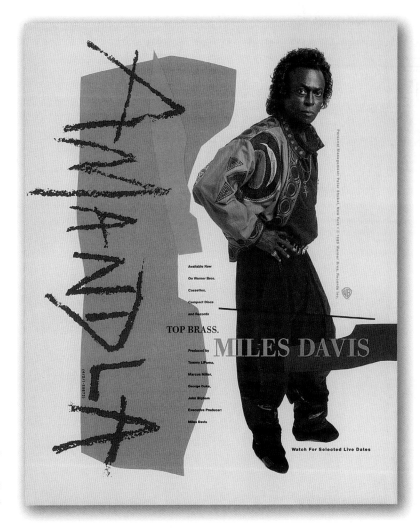

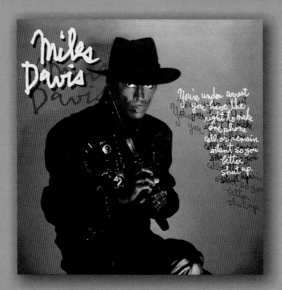

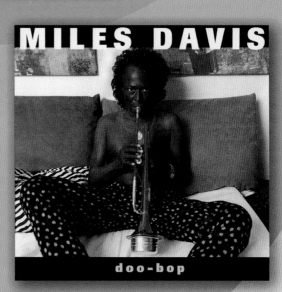

Few major jazz critics were conversant in Soul, Funk, Blaxploitation Cinema or Pan-Afrikanism back in 1972 so Miles' drift towards those vernacular palettes couldn't help but bewilder and bedevil the usual suspects at *Beat Down* (as certain mentors had renamed that deathless rag). Miles couldn't have cared less. He made 1970s Funk orchestration safe ground for serious improvisational exploration by his former associates. He provided coverage from critical attack without which Herbie Hancock might've been too chicken-shy to form Headhunters, or Zawinul and Shorter to go Weather Reporting.

Our Dark Prince had been inching his way towards The Funk for several years prior: on *Nefertiti*'s elongated, solo-free repetition of Shorter's plaintive melody over Tony Williams' Vesuvian eruptions one hears the template for everything to come. Miles being Miles he couldn't just copycat. He had to connect the dots between swing and Funk on his own terms. When one imagines all the cheap ways Miles could have accessed the cream of rock and soul to save his career, *Bitches Brew* and all that followed loom as totems of integrity. Dude might have been chasing rock star status but his methods harkened more towards Congo Square than Haight-Ashbury or Abbey Road.

The music Miles released in the early 1970s—on *A Tribute to Jack Johnson, Live-Evil, Miles Davis at Fillmore, On the Corner, Live at Philharmonic Hall, Big Fun, Get Up with It*—was of that funky time but miles ahead of it too. MD's funk was avant-esoteric even compared to freaky-deke Funkadelic. (Miles, of course, never needed lyrics to express his angst.) It exhibited way more corrosion on its acid-washed windowpane, sounded more frayed and bent at the fringe-leather edges. Lost in the defamations of his 1970s electronica is how dissonant and wounded his trumpet sound became as his music emulated the light-crushing gravitas of a black hole. While Hancock and Weather Report's funk turned sterile as the 1970s rolled on, Miles kept running the voodoo further down as if under orders of the meanest Benin and Dahomean gods. Only Fela and Lee Scratch Perry were producing funk as twisted, thorny, sardonic and ghettocentric as Miles was by the mid-1970s.

The blues also makes a strong resurgence in his writing and his trumpet work, especially on *Jack Johnson* and *Live Evil* and cuts like *Big Fun*'s "Go Ahead John," refracted from the same spiritual hellholes that inspired Marvin's "Inner City Blues," Scott-Heron's "Winter in America," and Marley's "Concrete Jungle." Like Albert Ayler, George Clinton, and Sun Ra, Miles seems to have understood that sounding incredibly earthy and extremely esoteric accurately mirrored both African American alienation and social reality. Black American music has always fluctuated between our desire for Dr. King's integrated America dream versus the desire to fully express what Malcolm X called our American nightmare. The blues, full of clashing tones that refuse to be resolved, unless diminished drives are present, comes roaring back in Miles' bleak and oblique horn breaks of the 1970s.

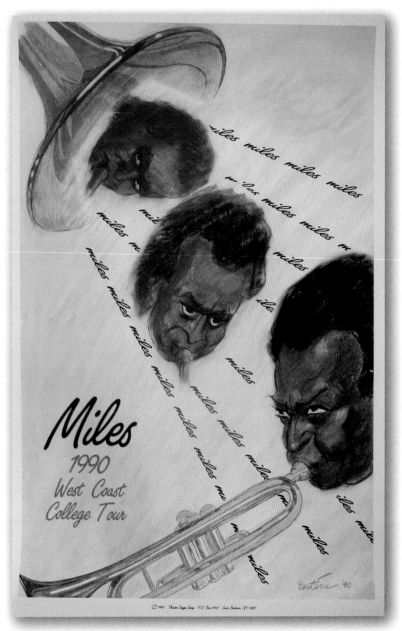

Poster, West Coast College Tour, 1990.

Miles can't be said to have fully embraced his funky potential until he hired Motown's own Michael Henderson to be his first, strictly Fender bassist after David Holland departed the band in 1970. Miles had famously said back in the 1960s that if the drummer ain't happening, ain't nothing happening. In the 1970s, the center shifted to Henderson's loping, low-end declensions, and the music took to swinging from the bottom up. When Henderson joined Miles those of us hooked on War, Funkadelic, and Santana took Miles to be their wiser, freakier gangsta-uncle from some Wagnerian Chicago juke joint underworld.

It's a statement on just how irrelevant acoustic jazz had become to young Black America that Henderson didn't know who Miles was when they first crossed paths. And when he got tapped to join dude's band and leave Stevie Wonder, he hadn't a clue that he'd be with Miles for almost six years. Throughout the multiple changes in personnel that occurred over the next five years Henderson remained the constant—the spine, gut, and anchor of the affair. The cornerstone experiments of the day—from *Live Evil* and *Jack Johnson* through *Dark Magus*, *Agharta*, *Pangaea*—would have collapsed without Henderson's mutable and motivic presence. He proved to be a savvy, elastic, improvisational groovemeister in the James Jamerson mold.

The 1970s turns out to have been the most adventurous and restless period of Miles' career. He composed almost all the music his bands played and was constantly blooming new color fields with a panorama of players, instruments, effects, and rhythms. Stylistically Miles prefigured many microgenres of the next thirty years—dub, punk-funk, new wave (that earstabbing Farfisa organ), hip-hop, trip-hop, industrial, electro, hardcore, drum'n'bass, grime, dub-step, even Bhangra—one listen to the tablas and sitars on *Big Fun* and *On the Corner* will break that connection down for you. I'm not waiting for Wynton Marsalis to make an album with Tricky but thanks to Miles it would certainly be in the tradition if he did.

I saw Miles for the first time not long after *Get Up with It* was released, at a defunct jazz club called The Etcetera on Washington D.C.'s M Street, when the band consisted of Henderson and three guitarists—Pete Cosey, Reggie Lucas, and Dominique Gaumont—plus Al Foster on drums, Mtume on percussion, and Sonny Fortune on saxes. Fortune, like Liebman before him, seemed to be there to provide a sonic link to the fluency and fury of Coltrane, the only obvious jazzy remnant Miles deemed fit for his newfangled jungle music. The real action were in the artful noises and polyrhythmic games being bandied about by Henderson, Mtume, and the seated, Buddah-like Cosey with his combination of multi-sonic guitaristry, mbiras, bells, and synthesizers. I remembered being enraptured by Miles working his wah-wah pedal, head and horn pointed down at the floor, playing brutal elephantine howls and violent banshee squalls that sounded like no trumpet I'd ever heard before or would ever hear again.

My jazz mentor Selim Garner remarked after one gig that Miles sounded like he had one foot in hell, but I've got more than musical memories to remind me of that week. My forty-five-year-old father, who came to hear Miles on a night that I missed, began suffering the first symptoms of what became a full-blown aneurysm by the time he reached the hospital. He survived it, praise Jah, surviving into a robust eighth decade he's enjoying today. But the forces invoked by Miles in 1974 were more than a Dantean metaphor for the kid after that. To hell and back he went to make his music happen, and damned if he wasn't going to try and take a few of us with him too.

Miles at the North Sea Jazz Festival, The Hague, the Netherlands, July 14, 1991.
Paul Bergen/Redferns

TIMING

by DAVE LIEBMAN

Saxophonist and flautist **DAVE LIEBMAN** played on three albums with Miles Davis as well as seven albums as a bandleader and numerous more as a sideman. In June 2010, he received a NEA Jazz Masters lifetime achievement award from the National Endowment for the Arts.

If I had to sum up Miles Davis in one word, he was about timing—in the musical sense, mostly playing those eighth notes directly in the middle of the beat and knowing when to hire someone new and make a change. Even in the dramatic pacing of his life, like those retrospective concerts he performed two months before he died, he knew when to do things—when and who and what to use in his music—and when to bow out . . . the ultimate producer/director. Everything he did, he did with an incredible sense of timing.

Miles had always been at the edge of the music, staying current, always searching. In the 1980s, when he was in his fifties and sixties, at times his health may have prohibited him from doing too much, but he took the time to do other things than music. He became more outgoing, more willing to share his knowledge and wisdom. He gave many interviews in those last few years and talked openly. He wrote his autobiography and got heavily into painting, at a pretty high level by the way. I felt that in his last ten years Miles was acting more like a grand master of the art than he ever had before.

My mother noticed an article in the *New York Times* that August saying Miles Davis was ill 1991, and the nature of the illness was undisclosed. For me, he was always in the hospital so that wasn't alarming. What was scary was to read that his ailment was undisclosed and that his family would not talk about it.

Miles had been touring all that summer right through the end of August. In July he had performed two serious events: one produced by Quincy Jones at the Montreux Jazz Festival that celebrated the music that Gil Evans and Miles did together. The other in Paris was even more special: a small group situation that focused on Miles and his former sidemen, from Jackie McLean up to Joe Zawinul, Wayne Shorter, John McLaughlin, Jon Scofield and Kenny Garrett, playing things like "All Blues" and "In a Silent Way." Then he received the Legion of Honor award from the French, their top award—it was a big summer.

This was truly a remarkable thing. Both had been retrospective concerts—something Miles had refused to do for many years. When he returned in the 1980s, he had been offered a million dollars in Japan to reunite with Herbie, Tony, Ron, and Wayne. He didn't. Instead it became the group VSOP, with Freddie Hubbard playing trumpet. Miles refused because it wasn't in his nature to look backward. He looked upon these retrospective events with skepticism, especially with him still being alive.

The day after Miles died there was a concert out here in Pennsylvania. My wife and I went to see Keith Jarrett, Jack DeJohnette, and Gary Peacock, Keith's regular trio, and it was a really great performance. After the show I went backstage and we were all sitting there shocked. Jack said, "The thing that we all got from him is 'Stay on course, and don't let anybody throw you.' " I said, "Have you heard anything about a funeral?" He said, "No. But they would have to have it in Madison Square Garden."

That Wednesday, I got a call from Jim Rose in George Wein's office. He had been Miles' road manager while I was in the band and for many years after. "It's an invitation-only memorial service. Can you come?" The service was at St. Peter's Church at 54th and Lexington, where Reverend John Gensel had presided over jazz memorial services for so many jazz players—Coltrane, Monk. It's a well-known church, very modern, almost non-denominational. The service was on that Saturday, a week after Miles died.

When I arrived, it felt like Hollywood. The press was lined up outside, lots of limousines. Inside, it was like Miles was there. They had gigantic pictures of him playing, of him receiving the medal from the Knights of Malta, of him looking great and smiling. It was so dramatic. It was also eerie in a way because it's a large church

OPPOSITE: Miles accepts applause at the Nice Jazz Festival in 1990.
David Redferns/Redferns

and they had the speakers on low, playing Miles' music, "All Blues" and other tunes, while the whole place was hushed. Everyone was quiet. I was sitting next to Monty Alexander. We just looked at each other and I said, "Oh God, this is so weird."

I looked around the room. I'd say there were four or five hundred people—quite a few I didn't know, and a lot of the musicians from my period with Miles whom I hadn't seen in twenty years, as well as Jack DeJohnette, Wayne Shorter, Dave Holland, and Herbie Hancock. We all had come to Miles when we were young and impressionable, not fully formed. For each of us, he had been our first big break. That bonded the fifty or so musicians attending who were lucky to have played with him over the past forty-five years.

David Dinkins, New York's mayor at the time, was the first of many speakers. He called Miles the quintessential New Yorker, saying that he had come from East St. Louis to attend Juilliard and lived here all his life. Quincy Jones talked about how Miles was his great idol way back in the 1940s and 1950s. Max Roach spoke about how they'd been together for years and how he helped Miles kick dope. Others talked about his influence, about his personality . . . how he was good looking, a great dresser, the cars, women, and boxing. They talked about how charismatic he was.

Bill Cosby, being Mr. Entertainer, was the best. He came up while people clapped for the speaker before him and lightened the atmosphere immediately: "It's OK to applaud," he said. "Miles is fine, everything is OK." Then he told some great stories. He said that news of what Miles did at 3:00 in the morning in a club in New York would get to Philadelphia by 3:30. The cats would all be running around talking about what he wore, what he played, who he hired, who he fired. Bill: "That's how important he was."

At one point, Cosby was saying that some people said Miles had AIDS. Then he said, "But in what order? It took fifteen things to knock this guy off." It was true. It was an incredible testament to Miles' strength. He was a frail person in some ways but in more ways he was very strong. There were always those two sides to him—he was a boxer who had a hip replacement, sickle cell anemia, diabetes. I heard that seven strokes in a twenty-four-hour period was the final bell.

I would say Jesse Jackson was the best speaker, I had never heard him speak live but immediately you could tell this guy was a trained speaker—loud, a preacher. His voice was like God. He gave a written eulogy. He finished with a beautiful poetic analogy for Miles. "He was our music man . . . blowing out of his horn, out of his soul" and so on. It was extremely uplifting.

Finally, Quincy got back up and said, "I'm going to show a little bit of this Gil Evans film from Montreux." At first it was so strange. Miles got up to play, he's smiling and waving, but there was no sound. Then the actual performance of "Summertime" came on. He played the melody and one chorus—and that was how the service ended after about one and one-half hours. I am sure everyone feared that it would be disorganized but in the end it was dignified and inspiring. It had not been a circus.

Afterward, everybody hung out, and it kind of cemented the bond between those of us who had actually worked with him. James Williams came by and said, "I guess school is out." Wayne Shorter is normally a man of few words, and speaks with a great smile on his face. He smiled and said, "I saw Miles just before he went to the hospital, and everything was OK. Don't worry." I felt that summed up what we all were feeling—which was that Miles left when he wanted to leave. Although he had only been sixty-five, he had lived a full life and he checked out at a good time. Look what the man left behind.

I agree with Wayne and Cos. It was not a tragedy—it was really OK. That was how I felt, and that's how I will feel forever I'm sure.

Miles requested that he be buried next to Duke Ellington in Woodmere Cemetery in the Bronx. I think it's fitting that they are together, because if anyone affected twentieth century music through the voice of jazz, it's definitely those two, and I would also add Louis Armstrong and Charlie Parker, all for bringing modern jazz into the world. They are all still head and shoulders above everybody.

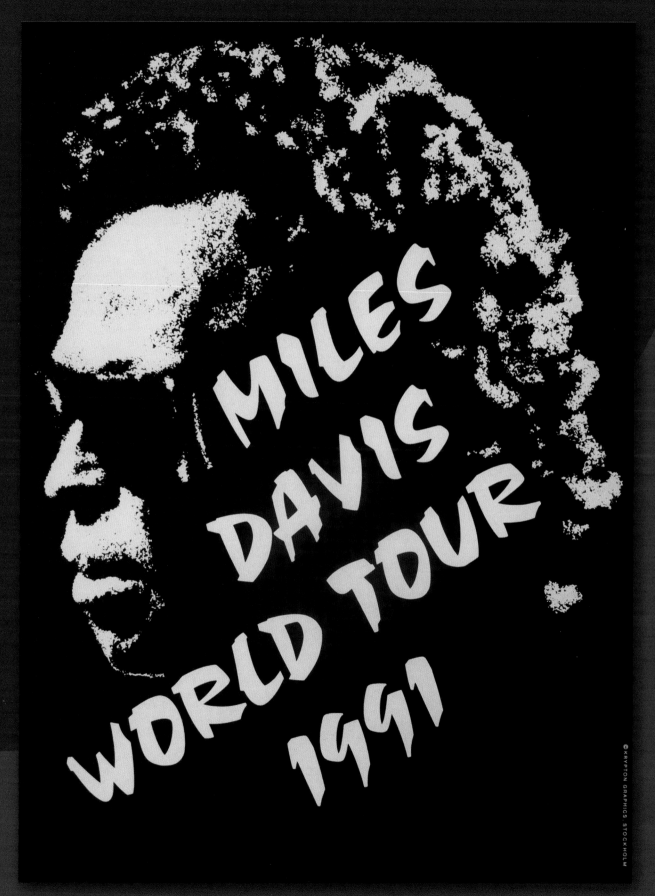

Poster, World Tour, 1991.

© KRYPTON GRAPHICS, STOCKHOLM

"I don't pay no attention to what critics say about me, the good or the bad. The toughest critic I got, and the only one I worry about, is myself. My music has got to get past me and I'm too vain to play anything I think is bad."

—Miles Davis, the *Playboy* interview, 1962

During his final tour, Miles plays the Royal Festival Hall, London, on July 1, 1991.
Tim Hall/Redferns